W9-AVS-309

This book is a gift from

_____

to

_____

because I care about you.

"NOT ME!"

How to PREPARE for Dangerous Encounters

AL HORNER

OTHER BOOKS BY AL HORNER

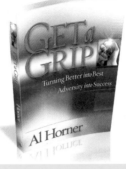

NOT ME!

by Al Horner

ISBN 1-932458-65-7

Published by Bronze Bow Publishing Inc.,
2600 E. 26th Street, Minneapolis, MN 55406.

You can reach us on the Internet at www.NotMeBook.com or www.BronzeBowPublishing.com

Cover/interior design by Koechel Peterson & Associates, Inc., Minneapolis, Minnesota.

Table of Contents

About the Author
AL HORNER

- Married to Diane for forty years.
- One son (Jason).
- Graduated from the University of Wisconsin with a BA and received an MBA (with honors) from the University of Minnesota.
- Served as an officer in the Underwater Demolition and SEAL Teams from 1969–1973.
- Was an international and commercial banker from 1974–1979.
- Led several businesses from 1980–1994.
- Acquired and has led Aaron Carlson Corporation since 1995.
- President of World Presidents' Organization, Twin Cities Chapter.
- President of North Central Chapter, UDT/SEAL Association.
- President of FBI Citizens Academy of the Twin Cities.
- Teaches the following courses:
    "Not Me!"—for women
        Permit to Carry a pistol certification
        Defensive and Tactical Pistol Training
- Author of *Get a Grip*

Dedication

This book is dedicated to each woman who has the wisdom to move past denial and the courage to resist when threatened.

Acknowledgments

Pat Fallon asked me to help prepare his daughter for the real world as she departed from home for college. What I created for her led to a self-protection course for girls and women and started this process.

The women of the Fallon agency used the courses' lessons as they faced threats over several years. Many of their stories are in this book. Thank you for your willingness to share sensitive information. Carree and Anna, your fingerprints are on this work.

Thank you to Christine Fruechte and the women of Colle McVoy who helped me create the title.

The caring people at Bronze Bow Publishing, especially Dave Koechel, John Peterson, Gregory Rohm, and Ryan Schmidt, supported this effort enthusiastically and did the design work.

Mark Kroskin, Christine Campbell, and Katie Aafedt led the way on Internet matters. Al Marrugi introduced me to the world of Internet book promotion.

Jan McDaniels, Judy Corson, Jeannie Joas, Chandler Cayot, Laura Kelly, Pam Sime, Laura Becker, Melissa Barnes, Mike Fiterman, and Dana Garry volunteered to help this material reach more women.

The wonderful work being done by Suzanne Koepplinger, Vednita Carter, and Patti Tototzintle for Native American, black, and Latin girls and women is an inspiration. A portion of the proceeds from this book will support their programs.

Dedicated professionals at the Federal Bureau of Investigation, including my friend Paul McCabe, are quiet heroes in the everyday battle to stop violent crime. The statistics generated by the Bureau help us deal with facts rather than conjecture.

My lovely bride, Diane, has consistently supported this effort to help women.

Heather Horner created the photography, and Samantha assisted. Amy McGarness put herself wholeheartedly into the photo shoots. Gail Joecks, Paul Morita, Michael Rogers, Cate Ford, Sarah Tollefson, Brittany Givens-Copeland, Jennaya Williamson, and Rick Plunkett were models for photos.

To each of these people, "Thank You," and I hope you understand that what we have created is making girls and women safer. It was worth doing.

Foreword BY ANNA STASSEN

Let's face it, there's no shortage of confidence among young women these days. We are in control of our lives, our careers, everything. Sometimes, though, that pumped-up confidence can bleed over into a false sense of security. We feel like we're invincible, and in most areas of life that's just fine. But when it comes to personal safety, our blinding confidence and denial of real threats can be a really dangerous thing because what we can't control, no matter how hard we try, are the actions of other people.

Through Al's class and this book, my friends and I have learned that we can't ignore the fact that when it comes down to it, men can still physically overpower us. If we have something they want, they can come and take it. Even if we're strong, we're still at a disadvantage. However, we can prepare.

There are ways to recognize risky situations and ways to get out of them when you find yourself smack-dab in the middle of danger. It's scary to think about, but even scarier to not. It was a rude awakening for me and many of my friends, and I'm thankful that Al taught us the tools we need to be safer.

chapter 1

What's
Real?

chapter 1

What's Real?

"Boys don't hit girls…men don't hurt women." It's an early life lesson that most men take seriously. But some don't. These bad guys are dangerous to girls and women.

Knowledge yields power. Let's increase your power by increasing your knowledge. To start, how much do you know about violence against women? Answer these questions as best you can. Mark your answers in the spaces provided so you can refer to them later.

Out of 100 women, how many are likely to be sexually assaulted during their lifetime? *Pick one.*

Fewer than 10 women   _____

10 to 15 women   _____

15 to 30 women   _____

Over 30 women   _____

Which age groups suffer the most sexual assaults? Rank these choices from 1 (most assaults) to 5 (fewest assaults):

Age 13 to 19 _____

Age 20 to 25 _____

Age 26 to 32 _____

Age 33 to 39 _____

Age 40+ _____

The woman will know the attacker in what percentage of assaults? *Pick one.*

Under 20% _____

25% to 50% _____

50% to 75% _____

75%+ _____

The male or female will have been drinking or using drugs in what percentage of assaults? *Pick one.*

Under 25% _____

25% to 50% _____

50%+ _____

What percentage of abductions by a stranger lead to assault, rape, or murder? *Pick one.*

50%+ _____   80%+ _____

60%+ _____   90%+ _____

70%+ _____

What percentage of assaults happen between dusk and dawn? *Pick one.*

Under 25%   _____

25% to 50%   _____

50% to 70%   _____

70%+   _____

Of women who fought, what percentage believe that their resistance improved the outcome (made things better)? *Pick one.*

Under 25%   _____

25% to 50%   _____

50% to 75%   _____

Over 75%   _____

 The quiz is about the big picture. Now let's focus on your personal reality.

REAL SCENARIO 1:
WHAT WAS THAT SOUND? THERE'S SOMEONE DOWNSTAIRS.

Lindsey was house-sitting for some friends. On a particularly windy night, she was getting ready for bed when she heard a loud noise. At first she told herself it was just the wind, perhaps a branch hitting the house. She carried on with her routine. Then, midway through brushing her teeth, she heard another noise. But this time it was followed by footsteps. She froze. Someone was in the house. And she was there alone.

REAL SCENARIO 2:
THAT MAN IS LOOKING AT ME WRONG. IT DOESN'T FEEL RIGHT.

Megan was walking to her downtown parking ramp after working late. It wasn't the greatest location, but the price was right for her early-'20s income. She got into the elevator and pressed floor 6. At floor 3, the elevator stopped, and the doors opened. A man was standing outside the door. He didn't get in; he just held the door open. "Do you have a light for my cigarette?" he asked her. She said no. But he still stood there, eyeing her up and down. Then he stepped into the elevator. Megan felt her stomach tighten. She needed to get away from this guy.

REAL SCENARIO 3:
OH NO! WE'RE ALONE, AND I DON'T WANT TO BE HERE.

Stephanie and Molly were in Spain on a vacation. They met a young local guy at a bar. He seemed nice enough, so they let him give them a tour of the city. Being a local, he knew the best places to go and the best ways to get there. By the end of the evening, he had become an insta-friend. But then he started getting grabby and affectionate. Stephanie and Molly passed it off as, "He's Spanish. They're affectionate people." He paid for the cab to get back to their hotel and then declared he was coming inside. Molly ran across the street to buy cigarettes while Stephanie and the young guy went upstairs. Once upstairs, he got aggressive. Almost forceful. Stephanie kept thinking, *Molly will be back soon, and I'll be okay*. Minutes passed and still no Molly. The guy pushed her down on the bed and ripped open her shirt. Stephanie began to cry, and he put his hand over her mouth to muffle the sounds.

If you haven't visualized what you would do in situations such as these, then you're in greater danger than you need to be. You are not prepared. You can be safer.

Fear of these scenarios is normal. Fear leads to denial. Denial leads to lack of preparation. ***Other than predators, a lack of preparation is your biggest enemy.***

In the pages ahead you will touch real-life experiences of women who faced dangerous men. Learn from their experiences. It takes courage to face these hard realities, but doing so will help you be safer.

You've already prepared yourself to handle many problems. For example, you probably know how to swim. That skill will help you survive if you fall into water unexpectedly. Knowing how to swim can't make you completely safe around water, but it can make you much safer. And understanding what to do during dangerous encounters with men will help you escape injury, rape, and death. The information in this book can't make you safe, but, like knowing how to swim, it can make you much safer.

IS THIS SOMETHING I REALLY NEED TO THINK ABOUT?

Let's look at statistics to understand the threats women really face. Statistics are abundant, and results vary from study to study, but consistent patterns emerge when results of many studies are compared. The ten generalizations below are derived from:

- "Violence Against Women: A National Crime Victimization Survey Report," U.S. Department of Justice, January 1994.

- "2005 Criminal Victimization in the U.S. Statistical Tables," U.S. Department of Justice.

- Observations from hundreds of women and girls who have attended my "Not Me!" training classes.

HOW MANY WOMEN GET ASSAULTED?

Between one in three and one in seven women will be assaulted during their lifetime. If a woman goes away to college, leaves home when she is a teen or young adult, or is from a minority, the number increases.

15% to 30% of females are likely to be assaulted

WHAT AGES ARE AT GREATEST RISK?

About 80% of assaults happen between ages 12 and 34, with the highest percentage of assaults on women in their late teens.

Girls and younger women are in greatest danger

WHO ATTACKS?

Most assaults (70%–80%) are committed by a man the woman knows.

Women often know the attacker

WHAT HAPPENS?

Assaults by non-strangers are damaging and tragic, but they are less violent than assaults by strangers. Over 90% of abductions by strangers result in serious harm or death to the woman.

Over 90% of abductions by strangers lead to tragedy

WHEN DO ATTACKS HAPPEN?

Most assaults (about 70%) happen between dusk and dawn.

Darkness is dangerous

ARE SOME ACTIVITIES MORE DANGEROUS THAN OTHERS?

In a majority of attacks (60%–70%), the attacker and/or the victim had been drinking or using some form of drugs.

A majority of attacks are linked to alcohol and drugs

WHERE DO ATTACKS HAPPEN?

Over half of all assaults occur in or around a woman's home or the homes of friends/relatives/neighbors. The next most likely place for attack is around your car.

50%+

Most assaults occur in residences and around cars

DO ATTACKERS USE WEAPONS?

Most attackers (80%) use personal force and do not use a weapon.

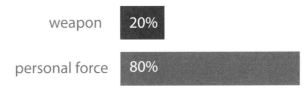

Most attackers don't use weapons

SHOULD I FIGHT OR COOPERATE?

Most victims (80%) that defended themselves believe their fighting was beneficial and reduced negative consequences.

About 80% of victims believe resisting helps

HOW MANY DANGEROUS MEN ARE OUT THERE?

There are about 250,000 rapists and sexual assault convicts in the U.S. On an average day about 150,000 of these men are out of prison on probation or parole. In addition to these convicts, there are many unconvicted predators in our communities.

[in hundred thousands]

About 150,000 of 250,000 convicts are on the street, and many more
attackers are present, but are never caught and convicted

LET'S DIG A LITTLE DEEPER INTO EACH OF THESE STATISTICS.

HOW MANY WOMEN GET ASSAULTED?

The most conservative research puts the victim rate at about one in seven. Some college student research tends to put the victim rate at closer to one in four. Among poor minority females the rate may be one in three.

Many assaults do not get reported, so the actual number of assaults is always higher than the reported number. When I teach "Not Me!" to young professional women, there are often two to four women in a group of twelve who admit having experienced an assault. That means that if you go to college or begin living away from home in your late teens and you have one sister and two girlfriends, one of the four of you is likely to be assaulted before you reach your early 30s. Anecdotal information from women that serve poor minority communities suggests that assault rates may be around one in three for women in this population segment.

WHAT AGES ARE AT GREATEST RISK?

Most studies start at age 12, but assault becomes significant at age 10. When young girls and their mothers attend "Not Me!" the innocence of the young girls is both wonderful and unnerving. Though girls in their early teens are exposed to sexual themes via the Internet and other media, the looks in their eyes tell me it is not personal yet. They don't understand how some boys and men see them. It's not until they get touched in a wrong way or see other girls being pawed at parties that they begin to understand the attraction their bodies have to males. Their innocence is, on one hand, a joy to see. On the other hand, it is distressing because it leaves them so vulnerable to predatory men and boys.

> Research results agree that assaults increase steadily from about age 10 through 20. The assault rate remains high in the early 20s and then trends downward until women reach their mid-30s. Though the incidence rate becomes lower after 35, it never reaches zero. Women are targets of assault throughout their lives.

WHO ATTACKS?

Most assaults are by a man the woman knows; between 20–30% are by a man the woman does not know. The most common violators include family members, friends, dates, neighbors, teachers, coworkers, and other men a woman knows and trusts. The number of non-stranger assaults is always underreported because girls and women don't notify authorities for a variety of reasons. There are also many unreported forced rapes and assaults by former boyfriends and husbands.

Anecdotal information indicates that a large number of young women are forced to have sex—date rapes—in their early dating experiences. Lack of information and inexperience can put the girl in a situation where she is isolated and vulnerable. Embarrassment causes her not to report the assault, so these date rape attackers get away with their assault.

WHAT HAPPENS?

Though attacks by strangers are less frequent than attacks by non-strangers, stranger attacks are more brutal and deadly.

When a woman knows the attacker, he expects to see her again in family, work, or community settings. If he visibly injures her, his risk of discovery increases, so assaults by non-strangers are typically less violent than assaults by strangers. Non-strangers also rely on women remaining silent because they feel humiliated and want to protect loved ones from bad news. Non-stranger assaults often follow a sequence such as this:

The woman trusts the man and talks to him. Somewhere along the way he establishes a connection with the woman that is closer than usual. He may say he has a problem he would like to discuss, or he may become an active listener as she talks about something she wants to share. One way or another he creates an interaction that is more personal than usual. Then he suggests they move to a more private location where they can talk without interruption. This may be upstairs, downstairs, in a car, in the yard, or anywhere else that separates them from other people. When he isolates her, he takes control and attacks.

So the process usually involves connecting in a way that is closer than usual and using that connection to achieve isolation. Connect, Isolate, and Attack.

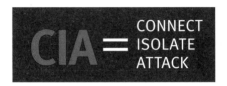

If a man you know tries to create a closer connection than usual, be cautious. If he tries to use that connection to isolate you and is insistent that you go with him, you are in a high-risk situation. Stop the process by refusing to be isolated. The wise choice is to remain within sight of friends if you choose to continue talking to him.

When a woman does not know the attacker, the outcomes are typically more violent. The following scenario is wrong in that it describes no particular attack, but right in that it is consistent with many stories I have heard.

The stranger trapped the woman in her home or apartment, or he abducted her near her car and transported her to an isolated location. Once she was isolated, potential rescuers could not hear her screams. He established control by forcing her to do things she did not want to do, such as disrobe or give him oral sex. Then he raped her or violated her in other ways. After he achieved his sexual release, he had to decide what to do with her. If he releases her, she is a liability and can testify against him. If he kills her, she can't testify.

Though exact statistics related to outcomes of stranger abductions are difficult to determine, I believe the following is roughly correct.

- About 40% of the time the woman is transported far from home or killed. Her loved ones never see her alive again. If she is killed, she most often dies within four hours of being abducted.

- About 50% of the time the woman is raped or seriously sexually abused.

- Less than 10% of the time the woman escapes or is released unharmed after abduction.

Less than 10% escape unharmed

Abduction by a stranger leads to tragedy over 90% of the time

These numbers have not been specifically validated in a study, but based on my research and experience, they are good approximations of reality. I believe that victims of stranger abductions experience horrible outcomes over 90% of the time.

A generally accepted statistic indicates that about two-thirds of the abducted women who are killed by strangers die within four hours of capture by their assailant. The sequence is: Abduct, Isolate, Attack. If any of these murder victims intended

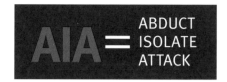

to reason with their abductors or receive sympathy from them leading to their release, there was very little time for that to happen. The women die within a few hours of abduction.

News stories that report victims establishing rapport with their abductors leading to their release or escape are dramatic and attractive to the media. But these stories do a great disservice to women because they obscure the statistical reality that about nine out of ten victims abducted by strangers experience horror or death.

To prevent attacks by strangers, stop the sequence at Abduct or Isolate by using precautions and escape techniques described in the chapters that follow.

WHEN DO ATTACKS HAPPEN?

Most attacks happen during the dark hours. These are times when women are at home, on dates, or partying. Though there are risks at school and work during the day, they are minimal compared to risks in less-structured evening environments, especially when assailants and/or victims have been drinking or using drugs.

WHERE DO ATTACKS HAPPEN?

There seems to be a correlation between the fact that most assaults are by a man the woman knows and the fact that most assaults occur in and around the woman's home or the home of friends/relatives/neighbors. Assaults happen when there is motive and opportunity. Motives vary from the assailant's desire for sexual gratification to a desire to control someone in his out-of-control world. Opportunity requires isolation, and homes or apartments offer privacy. If a predator is with a trusting woman and she allows herself to be isolated from help, the scene is set for him to attack.

DO ATTACKERS USE WEAPONS?

Department of Justice statistics indicate that assailants use weapons only about 20% of the time. About 80% of the time the attacker uses surprise and physical force against his victim. Though nothing about sexual assaults is good news, this statistic helps us see possibilities that we will develop into effective self-defense strategies.

SHOULD I FIGHT OR COOPERATE?

Department of Justice studies indicate that victims who fought the attacker believed they improved the outcome about 80% of the time.

Let's put this statistic together with other pieces of information to help answer the question about whether you should resist or not.

- About 2/3 of attacks are by men you know. They want to have sex, but they don't want to visibly injure you too badly. Implication: if you resist aggressively, he may back off rather than visibly hurt you or risk visible injury to himself.

- Most abductions by strangers (about 90%) result in horrendous outcomes. Implication: fight with all your might. If you cooperate and allow yourself to be captured and transported, the outcome is likely to be tragic. Even if you get hurt resisting abduction, that injury is likely to be less damaging than what will happen if he isolates you.

- Most assailants (80%) do not use weapons. Implication: since most attackers don't use weapons, you can learn a few simple actions that will surprise and hurt the attacker, allowing you to get separation from him and escape.

The simple answer to, "Should I resist or not?" is clear. Fight with everything you have! If you submit to a man you know, you will be raped or worse. If you submit to a man you don't know, the outcome will be torture, rape, disappearance, or death nine times out of ten.

You have to respond to an attack based on your assessment of the situation. Only you can decide what's best. The women whom I am close to have thought this issue through and decided they will fight with everything they have as soon as a man tries to capture, abduct, or transport them. They know the statistics; cooperation is a bad choice.

ARE SOME ACTIVITIES MORE DANGEROUS THAN OTHERS?
Absolutely. Partying, dating, and any other activities that involve use of alcohol or drugs are the highest risk activities.

The data on this topic show that about half of convicted sex offenders say they used alcohol or drugs prior to assaulting their victims. And this is just what the attackers did. If we look at the likelihood that attackers took advantage of women who drank too much or used drugs, it's easy to estimate that the percentage of assaults involving drinking or drugs is well above 50%.

When I ask women to describe how they change when they drink, they say:

> "I become less inhibited."

> "I become less aware of what's going on around me."

> "I get more cuddly or affectionate."

When I ask women to describe how men change when they drink, they say:

> "They become more aggressive."

> "They become less inhibited."

> "They get more interested in sex."

If women who are less inhibited, less aware, and more affectionate combine with men who are more aggressive, less inhibited, and more interested in sex, the situation is high risk for women. And if there are predatory men present who focus on women who have been drinking too much, those women are in real danger.

DANGER INCREASES GREATLY WHEN YOU PARTY WITH ALCOHOL AND DRUGS.

HOW MANY PREDATORY MEN ARE OUT THERE?

Here are some indicators:

- Department of Justice statistics indicate there are about 250,000 convicted rapists and sex offenders in the U.S.

- On an average day about 60% (150,000) of these convicts are out of jail on probation or parole in their communities.

- The median age of new male sex offenders is early to mid teens. Girls in their early and mid teens are living among boys who are the fastest growing group of new sex offenders.

- Recidivism is high (sex offenders tend not to be rehabilitated), so the new teenage boys who enter the assailant category cause a steady increase in the total number of potential attackers.

In addition to the known number of convicted predators, there are many unconvicted attackers—men who have assaulted women but have not been reported and apprehended.

So what does all this mean?

- **MURDER.** Every day four women die in this country as the result of domestic violence by husbands and boyfriends.

- **BATTERING.** Conservative estimates indicate that somewhere between 2 million and 4 million women are battered each year.

- **RAPE OR ATTEMPTED RAPE.** Between 400,000 and 900,000 women are raped each year. In addition, current or former male partners forcibly rape about 1,200,000 women.

This data is a reality check with no attempt to be dramatic. American women live in an environment that recognizes and promotes their individuality as persons, but also houses some men who just want to use their bodies. If you feel concerned and want to deal with this reality, congratulations. You're preparing to be safer.

In the chapters that follow, you can put yourself in the place of many women who faced threats. Immerse yourself in each real-world story because the story is linked to an important lesson. There is no better way to prepare for dangerous encounters than to live in each story, use the lesson, and visualize winning.

Prepare

UNDERSTAND REALITY, AVOID DENIAL, PREPARE YOURSELF IF

DANGER FORCES ITSELF INTO YOUR LIFE.

chapter 2

Men You Think
You Know

chapter 2

Men You Think You Know

Remember: 70%–80% of assaults are by a man the woman knows.

"Don't resist. I won't hurt you." He's lying. He just wants you to comply, and he's going to hurt you.

THE HOLIDAY PARTY

After leaving for college two years ago, Ann was back at home for the annual holiday family get-together. About halfway through the evening, she was sharing feelings with her cousin. He said that he had always felt comfortable with Ann and started telling her about some difficulties he was having. As the conversation progressed, he suggested they go downstairs to a more private area where they could talk with fewer interruptions and distractions. Ann agreed.

Once they got downstairs, he got aggressive. He pinned Ann down and pulled her skirt up. She struggled, but he said, "I won't hurt you if you cooperate. It will be terrible for everyone if you scream."

She stopped fighting. He raped her.

When it was over, he went back upstairs. Ann cleaned up and didn't tell anyone for fear of ruining the holiday party and tearing the family apart. Years later in a "Not Me!" session, she broke down as she told the story. He had hurt her deeply. Sharing what happened was a great relief for her because now friends knew the truth and could give her the support she needed.

Most women live in close contact with their compassionate, nurturing feelings. This tendency is wonderful in most scenarios, but in the presence of a male predator it can be dangerous. Be aware that a predator can use your sensitivity to trap you.

Predators interview women. The process helps the predator determine whether a woman will cooperate or fight during the assault, and whether she will report the assault or keep it to herself. Do you recall the likely assault sequence involving a man you know?

To prevent the Attack, stop the sequence at Connect or Isolate

If your senses of compassion and nurture lead you closer to a man as he connects with you, they may also lead you to isolation with him. Isolation creates his opportunity to attack. And if, after the assault, your priority is to spare loved ones pain, you may keep the attack to yourself.

Please continue to be guided by your compassionate, nurturing feelings. Our world needs these in large doses. But be aware of how your emotional tendencies can lead you into danger.

How can I know whether he is setting me up for attack or just wants to talk? Think about the place near your heart where you get that queasy feeling when you hear a police car or fire engine siren. You know. It's that quiet, subtle place that gets upset when things aren't right. That's where your personal Threat Alarm is located. Some say this place is linked to intuition. Whether you believe your Threat Alarm comes from intuition, guardian angels working to warn you about danger, or gut instincts based on eons of survival, that personal Threat Alarm is real. You have it. It activates when danger is near. The question is, "Do you listen to it?"

We'll discuss more about intuition and your Threat Alarm later, but for now just realize that your Threat Alarm exists. If you ask it, "Is there danger?" and trust the answer, it will give you information you need. If you ask the question and get either hesitation or a queasy feeling, do not get isolated with a man. Stop the CIA sequence to prevent the attack. You may choose to continue your conversation in a public setting, but do not let him distance you from the group.

If he is really interested in discussing the topic with you, he'll value your company enough to continue the conversation in the group setting. If he presses for isolation, get away from him.

And remember what happens when you drink—you become less inhibited, less aware, and more affectionate. If he is a predator, you may be in danger.

Trust your instincts and feelings if they tell you something isn't right.

PLAYING POOL

As a teenager, Peggy was a tomboy. She was strong and enjoyed playing sports with her guy friends. When she became a young woman, she dated masculine men and enjoyed competing playfully with her dates.

On one occasion, she and her date were having a few drinks at his house. He challenged her to game of pool. Rising to the challenge, she said it wouldn't be fair because she would beat him too badly. One thing led to another, and she found herself in his poolroom. As the game progressed, he made increasingly suggestive comments as she leaned over the table to make shots. Soon he was close to her. Trying to be tough, she focused on the game, telling him to back off. The situation didn't feel right, but she thought she could handle it.

Then he came up behind her, lifted her onto the table, and began to pull at her jeans. She told him to stop, but the only way she could get away was to hit him with the pool cue. That stopped him, and she ran out of the house as he nursed his bleeding cut.

These situations with men you know are difficult. You may not want to do something that makes the man feel bad. You probably know women who have faced situations such as this. Discuss those situations with them and learn from their experience. Talk about what feelings they had prior to an attack, what they did right, and what they wouldn't do again.

Remember that most assaults are by a man you know. Trust your instincts and get away from a man if anything feels wrong or unusual. Do not get isolated with him. And if you are attacked, report the attack so he can't hurt you or other women again.

Prepare

LISTEN TO YOUR INSTINCTS. IF SOMEONE YOU KNOW GETS CLOSER THAN NORMAL AND THEN TRIES TO FORCE YOU INTO ISOLATION, GET AWAY! STOP THE SEQUENCE OF "CONNECT AND ISOLATE" TO PREVENT THE ATTACK.

chapter **3**

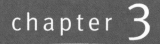

Staying
Alive

chapter 3
Staying Alive

REMEMBER:

About 80%
of victims
who resisted
believe it
improved
the outcome.
About 80%
of attackers
do not use
weapons.

REMEMBER: About 80% of victims who resisted believe it improved the outcome. About 80% of attackers do not use weapons.

Let's use these two pieces of information to your advantage. If you prepare to resist and have a weapon, you will be safer. Specific information about resisting and weapons follows, but first you need to understand how to mentally and emotionally transition from your normal world to the scenario where you face a threat.

COMBAT MIND-SET

The threat condition at the airport is Orange. What does that mean? If Orange tells you something about what the threat is and what you should do, then the color code system is useful. If it tells you nothing, then it is not useful. Let's create your personal threat color code system.

The system has four colors: White, Yellow, Red, and Black. Each color describes a specific circumstance, and each color calls for a specific response from you. By understanding the threat color code system, you prepare yourself to identify threats and react to them effectively. Here we go…

☐ **CIRCUMSTANCE:** You are in a very safe place, alone or with those you trust completely. This is la-la land. White is appropriate at your home and your parents' home if the only people present are loving members of your immediate family.

YOUR RESPONSE: It is okay to be totally relaxed and unaware of your surroundings. You can be in la-la land.

ASSESSMENT: There are few very safe places, but they are important because we all need rest, renewal, and places of unconditional love and acceptance. Enjoy your very safe places. Don't worry; be happy.

☐ **CIRCUMSTANCE:** You are in a very safe place, but someone you don't trust completely has come into the place. Now the place has changed; threats may be present. It has become like the world outside where unsettled people may do you harm. As soon as someone comes into your very safe place or as soon as you leave your very safe place, shift to Yellow.

YOUR RESPONSE: In Yellow you are relaxed and enjoying life, but you turn your Threat Alarm on so you can recognize potential threats. You simply recognize that threats may exist, and you ask your Threat Alarm to tell you when danger is near.

ASSESSMENT: Switching your Threat Alarm on does not mean you turn into James Bond, living in constant tension as you look for bad guys. In Yellow, you still enjoy looking at the blue sky, being refreshed as a cool breeze blows across your face, and feeling the warmth of loving souls around you. None of this is lost. But turning your Threat Alarm on allows you to recognize danger when it comes.

You can sense threats many ways. You may see or hear something that isn't normal or feel a touch that is unsettling. Intuition may tell you to be careful. Any of these inputs can activate your Threat Alarm. The question is whether you'll listen to the alarm or override it by thinking. When your Threat Alarm goes off, your mind is a terrible thing to use. Better to trust your intuition first and get away from the threat immediately.

SEEING WHAT YOU WANT TO SEE

Diane came from a happy home and lived in her happy teenage world. She felt safe and trusted people.

As she walked home from her summer job as a lifeguard, she approached a man standing on the sidewalk by his parked car. The car's trunk was open, and the man had on a long coat.

Why is his trunk open? she wondered. *He must be loading his car for a picnic,* she thought. *But where is his picnic stuff? Hmmm.*

Why is he wearing a long coat during the summertime? she thought. *Maybe he thinks it's going to rain. But it's sunny. Hmmm.*

Why is his trunk open? Why is he wearing a long coat in the summertime? She pondered these two questions as she walked toward him.

It wasn't until she got close to him and he opened his coat, exposing himself, that she allowed herself to believe something was wrong.

She ran as fast as she could. The man jumped into his car and chased her down the block. Desperate for help, she ran around a corner and up to a house. She opened the storm door and sandwiched herself between it and the inside door. The man's car came around the corner. Whether he lost sight of her or just lost his nerve, he drove past the house and kept going. After she was certain he was gone, she ran the rest of the way home.

Denial can cause you to overthink what you are seeing. Diane saw a man in her path. He was wearing a long coat on a hot summer day. He was standing by a car with its trunk open for no apparent reason. Rather than recognize these facts as unusual and potentially threatening, she tried to rationalize what she saw. She was thinking. She got dangerously close to him. Only when he exposed himself and came toward her did she recognize the threat.

As a young woman, she didn't understand that she was in a dangerous period of her life. She didn't associate cars with increased levels of risk. And she wasn't aware that she had a Threat Alarm that she could trust. She was living in White when she should have been in Yellow so she could recognize the threat early and stay away from it.

Remember that denial is potentially your biggest enemy. Going into Yellow is about recognizing that you have a personal Threat Alarm, switching it on when you leave your very safe place, and avoiding denial when your Threat Alarm goes off. Your Threat Alarm can go off in response to a person, place, car, party, street, house, path, building, or many other triggers. When it goes off, don't think—just get safe separation from what feels wrong. After you are safe, allow yourself to analyze the possible causes, but get safe first.

WHAT FRIENDS ARE FOR

Anne and Courtney were celebrating their 30th birthdays in Italy. They found a place called "The American Bar" and decided they were in the mood for some good old American rock music and people who could speak English. They met a lot of interesting Americans who had all landed in the bar that night. It was a blast.

After a couple hours of adult beverages and interesting conversation, Anne noticed that Courtney had moved out into the alley behind the bar with a group of guys. Being tall and blonde, Courtney was always a hit with the boys. Anne went out to see if she was okay. Courtney said she had just kissed one of the guys. He was a surfer. She was infatuated. But it didn't feel right to Anne. She didn't trust these guys. So she stayed in the alley with Courtney and her new "boyfriend."

Minutes passed, and all of the sudden Courtney began severely slurring her words. Her eyes weren't focusing, and she was clumsily dropping her money on the ground. A group of men circled in like vultures to "help" her pick it up. Anne went into protection mode. She didn't like this at all. She felt a mild panic come on. They'd been drunk together before. Very drunk, in fact. And this was not "drunk Courtney."

Anne told the guys to back off. The men were persistent and a little too eager to help. She put Courtney's arm over her shoulder, and they started walking the three-quarter's mile back to their hotel. As they walked back, Courtney got worse and worse. She threw up a couple times. Anne was just glad they got out of there. Who knows what would have happened if they hadn't?

The next day Courtney woke up refreshed, but missing a few hours from the night before. She had been drugged. But she was home safe. Anne's intuition had saved them from something bad.

Make the following connection:

THREAT ALARM = GET AWAY

You don't need to wait until a person has cornered you or has touched you. Trust your instincts...get away!

REALITY CHECK. THIS IS IMPORTANT. Realize that when your Threat Alarm goes off in Yellow, you may face a difficult decision...a critical moment. In that moment you may feel embarrassed about moving away from a person or a place based just on a feeling, but your alternative is to ignore the feeling and put yourself at risk. This boils down to two choices:

CHOICE A: Immediately move away from anyone who feels like a threat—even when it's embarrassing.

CHOICE B: Don't move away and put yourself at risk of rape or worse.

Trust your intuition and your Threat Alarm...get away! Remember the statistics. One of every three to seven women will be assaulted. If a stranger abducts you, the results will nearly always be very bad. Moving away from a person or place may be embarrassing, but if your instincts, intuition, or Threat Alarm are warning you, then getting away is much wiser than risking assault. So trust your instincts and get away!

JUST GET AWAY

Emily and her friends frequented a bar close to their office. They knew all of the bartenders. They knew all of the regulars. It was a comfortable home-away-from-home for them.

One night Emily was talking to one of the regulars, Chip. He was a lawyer who worked across the street. They had talked many times before, and she had heard stories about his troubled marriage, his children, and his frustrations with his job. Emily just thought he needed a friend, and she was glad to be someone with whom he could talk. But that night the conversation turned. Chip wanted to know about Emily's sexual experience. She made a joke and passed it off as innocent flirtation. But Chip kept at it. Then he asked her to go with him to the back parking lot because he wanted to show her something. Emily was worried that if she kept saying no, he'd be offended. And he was a regular, so she'd definitely see him again. But she stayed put.

He tried, and tried, and tried to lure her to the parking lot, and she finally said no. He leaned in close and whispered in her ear, "I'm going to give you five orgasms." Her first thought was *Why five?* and her second thought was *I have got to get out of here.* So she went with the second thought and told him she had to use the ladies room. When his back was turned, she slipped out the front door of the bar and jumped into a cab.

■ **CIRCUMSTANCE:** You recognized the threat and tried to get away, but you couldn't. You are trapped.

YOUR RESPONSE: Decide if you are going be a victim or not. If you cooperate, you will be a victim. If you freeze, you will be a victim. If you say, "Not Me!" you may get hurt resisting, but you're avoiding torture, rape, or death. Let's make this clear and simple:

> **CHOICE A:** Say, "Not Me!" and get hurt while resisting.

> **CHOICE B:** Suffer torture, rape, or death by submitting.

Neither choice is great, but one is clearly better than the other. Don't submit. Choose to fight with all your might.

ASSESSMENT: Denial is still your worst enemy. If fear causes you to deny the presence of the threat, you may delay action. Delaying action gets you deeper into the situation.

Understand that anyone under attack is afraid. Saying, "Don't be afraid" is like saying, "Don't be 5'6" tall." You are either 5'6" tall or you're not. You don't have a choice. If you are afraid, you are afraid. You don't have a choice. But there is a way to beat fear.

Courage is the antidote to fear. You can achieve courage by thinking in advance about how you will handle a scary situation and deciding what you are going to do. The more times you visualize yourself doing something with a successful outcome, the more courage you will have to take the action if you really need to.

Another way to think of this critical moment is: "You'll play the way you practice" and "You'll fight the way you train." If you visualize what you'll do in threatening situations and then add a dose of courage, you will respond properly.

VISUALIZE TAKING IMMEDIATE ACTION AND ESCAPING

PACKING FOR SCHOOL

She was finally doing it. Maggie was leaving for college. Excitement and anxiety filled her mind as she leaned over the bumper of her car.

"How am I going to get all my bags in this small trunk?"

She was snapped back into the moment as a hand ran up her leg and lifted her skirt. She spun and faced the man. Her first reaction was paralyzing fear.

What should I do?

She flashed back to what she had learned in her "Not Me!" class and thought, *Not me! I am not going to be a victim!*

She remembered "the cat move." Screaming "No!" she jabbed both hands at the man's eyes. Though she can't remember if she actually got his eyes, she knows he backed up, and she was able to run away into her house.

What may have become a tragedy is now just an unpleasant story, because Maggie had previously decided that she was not going to be a victim. Though she was terrified, she took immediate action.

The key in Red is to decide if you are going to fight or not. If there is doubt in your mind about what to do, look at the statistics again and get in touch with reality.

Let's create the transitions from White to Red in your world. You have left your very safe place and are in Yellow, enjoying the world with your Threat Alarm turned on. You go through a normal day. After work you walk to your car, parked in a ramp. It's about dusk. You step off the elevator, and the doors close behind you. As you look toward your car, you see a man. He is not getting into or out of a car; he is just hanging around. Your Threat Alarm goes off. You quickly determine that you can't get to your car before he can get to you. You immediately try to get back on the elevator, but the doors are closed. You look toward the stairwell, but it's too far away. The man begins moving toward you. You are in Red, and it's time to decide if you are going to fight or cooperate if he threatens you. You remember the statistics on attacks by strangers, and you decide that cooperation is victim behavior and there is no way you will cooperate if this man attacks. You have visualized a situation such as this, and you know you have choices if he tries to grab you. You will not let him capture or transport you. This public place is where you are going to make your stand if he attacks.

BLACK ☠

CIRCUMSTANCE: You are trapped and fighting for your life. There will be a winner and a loser.

YOUR RESPONSE: You must escape from him. The first few seconds are critical. At first contact, you will use surprise and overwhelming force to proclaim that you are not going to be a victim. Do not get captured. Do not get transported.

ASSESSMENT: Most attackers are looking for victims—women who will submit and allow the attacker to have control. If you scream and use the actions in this section, the attacker will know he is in for a fight. Frequently he will end the assault because he is looking for a victim, not a fight.

We had a saying in the SEAL Teams, "If you are in a fair fight...your tactics are bad." Make your resistance effective, using surprise and overwhelming force. Screaming is an important part of surprise; attacking his eyes is an important part of overwhelming force.

WHY SCREAM?

There are three reasons to scream as loudly as you can when you resist:

1. Loud screaming will surprise your attacker and help convince him that you are not going to be an easy victim.

2. Screaming is a cry for help. The initial attack will probably occur in the most public place you will be with the attacker. As soon as he grabs you, he will begin trying to isolate you from help. Your scream is most likely to be heard by people in that first, most public, place.

3. Screaming will put more power into your strike (we'll learn about the strike soon). Martial artists and tennis players know that if they yell, they put more energy into their body movements. The same will be true for you. When you make your move, scream because it will put more energy into your attack.

ON VACATION

It was the middle of winter when Carree and her girlfriend left the frigid north to vacation for a week. Sunshine, warm water, and sand beneath her feet...it was everything she wanted.

She woke up one night, had trouble going back to sleep, and went downstairs to gaze at a sailboat cruising on the ocean. Outside she heard a noise. *It's probably the security guard,* she thought.

Moments later a man came through the patio door with a machete in his hand. Carree froze. He forced her onto the couch. As he was removing her pajamas, she visualized her husband's face and agonized over what she was going to say to him. Then she saw my face saying, "Don't be a victim!" Her mind clicked into gear...*Not me!*

Knowing she was likely to get hurt, she screamed, grabbed the machete blade with one hand, and jabbed her fingers into the attacker's eyes with her other hand. The startled attacker backed off and ran out the door.

Carree and her husband came to my office and told this story in front of my wife and our employees. Her hand was wrapped in a large gauze bandage. When she finished the story, I asked her if she was sure she wanted to say "Thank you," given that her hand was badly cut. We were all teary as she said that the cut on her hand was minor compared to what was going to happen if she didn't resist.

First, Carree chose to ignore the noise outside (denial). Then she was so scared that she briefly took her mind somewhere else to escape the horror she faced (normal fear). But she had made her "Not me!" decision prior to the assault (preparation). She summoned the courage to take action using the two critical elements—surprise and overwhelming force. Her combination of screaming, grabbing the machete, and jabbing the attacker's eyes startled him, and his response was to retreat. Mission accomplished! Congratulations, Carree. You won!

DON'T EVER GIVE UP!

IF YOU GIVE UP,
YOU LOSE.

Who is going to win? Are you betting on the heron? Are you betting on the frog? I don't know who is going to win, but I know who is going to lose. **Whoever gives up first will lose! Do not give up. Do not get captured. Do not get transported.** If you only remember one thing from this book **remember this, "Never give up!"**

IF YOU HAVE TO FIGHT, STRIKE WITH OVERWHELMING FORCE AT HIS EYES

The average man is stronger than the average women. Usually, if a woman fights with a man, she loses. So don't get into a fight with a man. Rather than fight with a man, get away from him, using surprise and overwhelming force through the cat move.

What's the cat move? Think of a hostile encounter between a cat and a dog. What happens first? As soon as the cat faces a hostile dog, the cat runs away (the cat is in Yellow, senses the threat, and gets away). But if the dog corners the cat, the cat chooses to defend itself (the cat is in Red, chooses not to be a victim, and prepares to fight). Then the cat maneuvers itself to prepare for the attack while hissing and screaming (the cat is making it clear there is going to be a fight and frequently the dog backs down rather than continue). If the dog doesn't back down, the cat waits until the dog's eyes and nose are within striking range, and then it lashes out. Screaming, the cat's claws tear at the dog's sensitive eyes and nose. When the dog pauses or retreats, the cat runs away and doesn't stop until it's safe. This is the cat move. In its simplest form: surprise him with a violent strike to his eyes as you scream loudly. When he reacts to your strike, he will back away. As he tends to his eyes, you run and scream until you are safe.

Throughout this section on fighting, remember that when in doubt, default to the cat move. Get in a position where you can surprise him with a violent strike to his eyes so you can escape while he deals with the pain.

If the attacker is approaching you and you see him coming, get away if possible. But if you are trapped, position his face in front of you and then strike.

HOW SHOULD YOU STRIKE?

Thrust into soft eye tissue. To do the move, extend your fingers on each hand and make them rigid rods with your fingertips slightly separated. You now have ten mini-spears that can penetrate sensitive tissue as you jab them through the surface of the attacker's face. The deeper you jab, the more stopping power you have. The thought of skewering an attacker's eye is certainly distasteful, but it will stop him long enough for you to escape.

If the thought of doing this is too unpleasant, then go back to Red right now. Decide whether you are going to be a victim or not. If you decide to hesitate or cooperate, that is victim behavior, and statistically the consequences for victims are tragic. If you decide not to be a victim, you are saying to yourself, "I am prepared to get hurt resisting (you may sprain or break a finger doing the cat move) rather than get raped or murdered by this guy."

MAKE YOUR DECISION NOW AND BE CLEAR TO YOURSELF ABOUT WHAT YOU HAVE DECIDED

If you decided not to be a victim, it's time to discuss effective ways to strike your attacker so he backs away and you can escape. Remember that you do not want to fight with the attacker; you want to create pain so he will back off and you can escape.

IF HE COMES AT YOU FROM THE FRONT:

 THERE ARE TWO POSSIBILITIES. In both cases, when his eyes are within striking range, use surprise and overwhelming force in your strike at his eyes.

If he gives you an opening to directly attack his eyes, do it with all your might as you scream as loudly as you can. See the picture sequence below. The woman is driving her fingers into the attacker's eyes with all her strength as she screams at the top of her lungs. If even one or two fingers get to his eyes, he will feel enough pain to pull back. That's when she escapes. She runs until she reaches safety.

CAT MOVE

If he pulls you close and blocks a direct path to his eyes, then reach over his arms and grab his ears with your fingers. (See the pictures below.) When you grab his ears, your thumbs can be positioned directly over his eyes. Gouge his eyes and scream. Even if only one of your thumbs reaches the target, the attacker will feel enough pain to pull back and protect his eyes. That's when you escape, running and screaming until you reach safety.

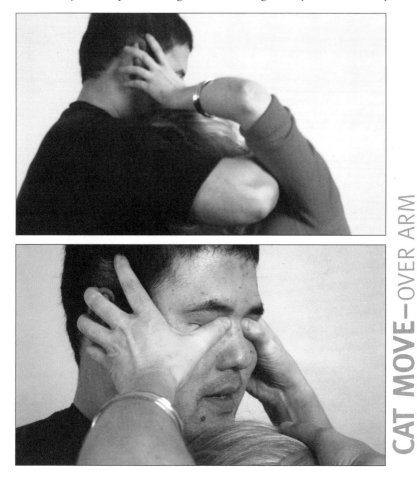

CAT MOVE–OVER ARM

IF HE COMES AT YOU FROM THE SIDE:

An attacker who grabs you from the side will likely pin your arm on that side against you so you can't attack with it. It is likely that your arm on the opposite side will not be immobilized. That opposite side arm becomes your weapon as you do the cat move with your fingers on that hand. (See the picture below.) If he has grabbed you, he will be close. Drive the fingers of your free hand into his eyes with all your might and scream. If any of your fingers find his eyes, he will feel enough pain to pull back. That's when you escape, running and screaming until you reach safety.

CAT MOVE—FROM SIDE

IF HE GRABS YOU FROM BEHIND:

 ATTACKS FROM BEHIND ARE THE MOST DIFFICULT TO HANDLE, but there is an effective method for escaping.

Any resistance is better than no resistance, but some actions are more effective than others. Less effective actions are:

- **ELBOWING.** Striking the attacker in his midsection with your elbows is better than nothing, but these are not immobilizing blows.

- **STOMPING ON HIS FOOT.** If he has grabbed you around your neck and is choking you, this action doesn't work because you can't see his feet.

- **SMASHING THE BACK OF YOUR HEAD INTO HIS FACE.** This can be effective if you hit his nose, but this action is often ineffective because you can't see your target if he's behind you.

- **GOUGING HIS EYES WITH YOUR FINGERS.** If you can get to his eyes, this variation on the cat move can be effective, but if you can't see his eyes, it may be hard to find your targets.

So what works the best? The most effective move is picking your legs up so he has to support your weight as he tries to move you.

The attacker usually wants to capture you and transport you to a more isolated location. Make it very hard for him to move you. Many videos of abductions show the attacker grabbing the victim and the victim resisting with her arms but moving her feet as the victim abducts her. These victims are unwittingly helping the attacker by supporting their own weight. DO NOT SUPPORT YOUR WEIGHT! Make it hard for the attacker by lifting both your legs off the ground (get your knees up to about 90° from your torso) and struggle with all your might. When you surprise him with this move, he will lose his balance and start to stumble forward. Be ready. As he loses his balance forward, put your feet down, break away, and run to escape from him. Run and scream until you reach safety.

YOU MAY HAVE TO DO THIS MOVE MORE THAN ONCE. THAT'S OKAY; DO IT. WEAR HIM OUT. DURING THE PROCESS, YOU MAY GET A SHOT AT HIS EYES— STRIKE IF YOU GET THE CHANCE.

LEG LIFT—GET AWAY

WHEN YOU RESIST LIKE THIS, TWO THINGS HAPPEN:
You are declaring that you are not a victim, plus you are forcing him to work very hard. He probably just wants a victim, and he probably doesn't want to work hard. You suddenly become much less appealing.

If he is choking you from behind so hard that you feel as though you will pass out, there is a tactic that can work. It is difficult psychologically, but it may be your best alternative. You must shift from fighting with all your might to being passive and acting like a victim. Stop fighting. When you quit resisting, the attacker will likely respond by loosening his grip. If you then use words such as, "Please don't hurt me" and "I'll do whatever you want," he may believe that he has won and you will cooperate. If your "victim" behavior gets him to come around in front of you, set yourself up for the cat move. Surprise him with your violent strike—scream and attack with all your might. If any of your fingers connect with his eyes, he will back off and respond to the pain. That is your opportunity to escape.

OTHER WAYS TO ATTACK

Always default to the cat move and strike the attacker's eyes, creating pain so he backs off and you can escape. Having said that, you should also be aware of other attack moves that can be effective if you can't get your fingers to the attacker's eyes.

BITING

Other than attacking eyes, this may be your most valuable tactic. It's disgusting to think about, but it's very effective when the alternative is rape or death.

If he is forcing you to have oral sex, bite down hard. If he is kissing you, bite his tongue hard. If your mouth is near his neck or face, bite as deeply as you can. In each case, he will react to pain and give you a chance to escape. Striking his eyes is always your first choice, but biting is an effective second choice.

THE FOLLOWING MOVES ARE LESS EFFECTIVE THAN THE CAT MOVE, BUT THEY CAN BE EFFECTIVE IF YOU CAN'T GET AT HIS EYES:

HEEL OF YOUR HAND

If you drive the heel of your hand into the attacker's nose, he will feel great pain and is likely to release you. Though this is an effective strike, you can usually do a cat move to the attacker's eyes from the same position. Default to the cat move to keep things simple.

HEEL OF HAND TO NOSE

ELBOWS ARE POWERFUL

If you can see the attacker's nose over your shoulder, he is
vulnerable to a blow from your elbow. In this move you strike
backward with your elbow as you simultaneously rotate your
body in the same direction. Rotating your body puts big muscles
into play and results in a powerful blow. If you can connect with
the attacker's nose, he will feel so much pain that he will back off.
This gives you an opportunity to escape. The move is effective if
you connect, but it is sometimes difficult to connect when your
target is hard to see over your shoulder. Use a cat move whenever
possible; use an elbow only when you can't use a cat move and
the attacker's nose is visible over your shoulder.

ELBOW TO NOSE

KNEEING IN THE GROIN

This all-time classic move is effective if you can pull it off. The problem is that men are well aware of this move, and they maneuver to avoid it. If the attacker pulls you very close, it's hard to get your knee up. If the attacker holds you at a distance, your knee won't reach him. The knee-to-groin only works well when the attacker is right in front of you and is close, but not too close. Attackers are much more likely to avoid this position than they are to protect themselves from a cat move. You'll be safer if you look for a cat move opportunity that will allow you to strike his eyes with surprise and violent force.

BREAKING A WRIST GRAB

If an attacker grabs you by one wrist, you can almost always get away. Here's how:

- Look at his hand and see his thumbnail.
- Simultaneously rotate your wrist toward his thumbnail and do a fast arm curl.

Here's what happens. By rotating your wrist toward his thumbnail, you are pitting your large arm muscles against his thumb muscles. Your arm muscles are stronger than his thumb muscles. When you do your fast arm curl, you will lever your wrist out of his thumb's grasp. The keys are to simultaneously rotate your wrist toward his thumbnail (not into his other four fingers) and do a fast arm curl, bringing your hand up to your own shoulder. (See pictures on next page.)

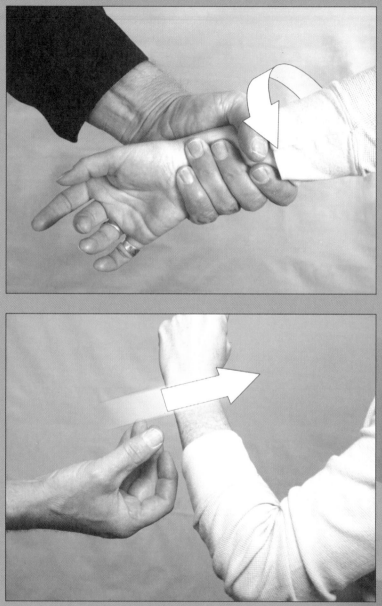

The two most common mistakes are rotating your wrist into his fingers rather than toward his thumbnail and pulling your whole arm away from him rather than doing a fast curl that brings your hand to your shoulder. Practice this move by getting a friend to grab your wrist firmly. Get a feel for the move by rotating your wrist toward his thumbnail and doing a fast arm curl. Unless there is a huge disparity in size and strength between the two of you, you will pry your wrist out of his grip no matter how hard he tries to grasp you.

ALWAYS RAISE YOUR HAND

TOWARD YOUR SHOULDER

GUNS AND KNIVES

Statistics tell us a small percentage of attackers use weapons. But if you're on the receiving end of an attacker's gun or knife, you can become paralyzed with fear. The short version of success dealing with a weapon is, "Get away from it." That takes courage. Remember that courage can come from rehearsing winning in your mind. Let's help you rehearse.

Several studies show that about 90% of police officers' shots are at threats seven yards away or closer. And of those close-range shots, only about one in ten shots actually hits the threat. Does this mean that police officers are terrible shots? No. It means that it is difficult to hit a person when adrenaline is pumping, the shooter is moving, and the target is moving. The same thing that is true for police officers is true for attackers—if they shoot at you from more than several yards distance, it is likely they will miss you.

Is it scary to think about someone shooting at you? Absolutely! It's terrifying!

Is it smart to think about what you'll do if someone shows a gun to attack you? Absolutely. It will prepare you to survive.

IT'S THIS SIMPLE,

"GUN, RUN."

GUN, RUN.

Unless the attacker has you in his grasp, immediately run as fast as you can. If you surprise him by screaming and running and he pauses, you will be getting to the range where he will have difficulty hitting you, even if he wants to draw attention to the situation and fire the gun. Your alternative is to freeze and let him capture you. If a stranger captures and transports you, the odds are about 90% that you will die, or something terrible will happen to you. This is one of those horrible moments that none of us wants to think about. And it's a critical choice time again:

CHOICE A: Immediately run away at first glimpse of any gun.

CHOICE B: Pause, get captured, and suffer through torture, rape, or death.

It's an easy choice. Imagine this moment in your mind and see yourself immediately running as soon as you see a pistol, before the attacker can capture you.

"GUN, RUN."

SEE IT. SEE IT AGAIN.

The exact same rules apply to knives. If an attacker shows a knife while he is not actually holding you, the best immediate response is to get more space between you and him.

"KNIFE, RUN."

If you pause and he grabs you, he has control. If he isolates the two of you, the statistics are terribly against you. If you see a knife, get space between you and him immediately. Don't think. Run as fast as you can.

"KNIFE, RUN."
VISUALIZE IT. PRACTICE IT IN YOUR MIND.

Do you see yourself immediately running as soon as you see a gun or knife? Please visualize doing this and be prepared.

In the case of both guns and knives, if the attacker is too close and you can't get away, then use courage and your wits to position him for the cat move or the use of any object that will inflict maximum pain on his eyes so he will back off, allowing you to escape.

Rehearse your reaction in your mind. You'll play the way you practice, and you'll fight the way you train.

Prepare

LISTEN TO YOUR THREAT ALARM. IF IT GOES OFF, GET AWAY FROM THE THREAT IMMEDIATELY. GUN, RUN. KNIFE, RUN. IF YOU MUST FIGHT, USE THE CAT MOVE WITH SURPRISE AND VIOLENT FORCE SO YOU CAN ESCAPE.

chapter 4

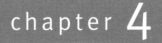

Weapons

chapter 4
Weapons

REMEMBER: About 80% of victims that resisted believe that their resistance was beneficial.

- About 80% of attackers did not use a weapon.

- 80%–90% of attackers who face a pistol discontinue the attack without a shot being fired.

SHOULD I USE A WEAPON OR NOT?

Your objective is to escape from, not fight with, an attacker. By showing a weapon (weapon includes more than just a gun as we'll discuss later in this chapter), making eye contact with him, and simultaneously retreating, you are presenting a strong presence as you move toward safety. Look him in the eye, show your weapon, and retreat. If he is looking for a victim, you are encouraging him to look elsewhere. The more convinced he is that you will fight aggressively, the less likely he is to continue his attack. He may pause. That creates your chance to escape.

Let's review a likely sequence of events to understand how to use a weapon.

- **IF YOUR COMMON SENSE SUGGESTS THE POSSIBILITY OF A THREAT,** have your weapon in your hand. Attacks happen fast. There probably won't be time to dig a weapon out of your purse if it is needed. As you walk into a parking lot, get into the elevator at a parking ramp, or walk down a street, pause and get your weapon in your hand. Your hand can be in your pocket or purse, but the weapon should be in your hand so you can use it instantly if necessary.

- **IF YOU SEE OR SENSE A POTENTIAL THREAT,** immediately move away from it. Get separation to a safe distance and then think about how to proceed.

- **IF AN ATTACKER IS CLOSING DISTANCE OR TRYING TO CUT OFF YOUR ESCAPE ROUTE,** look him in the eye, show your weapon, and retreat by the fastest route to safety. Through eye contact, your attitude, and the presence of the weapon, convince him that whatever he is contemplating won't be easy because you will fight like crazy!

- **IF YOU CAN'T ESCAPE AND ARE FORCED TO FIGHT,** pick your time and then strike his eyes/nose/face as violently as you can. Strike him aggressively so he feels great pain, forcing him to pause. That creates your opportunity to escape.

Remember that the first contact place, the most public place, is the place to make your stand. Scream, use your weapon to strike his eyes, then escape.

Some of the weapons described below are very intimidating; others are less so. All of these weapons are better than nothing when you are convincing an attacker that you will not be a victim and he is in for a fight if he gets close to you.

YOUR WITS AND COURAGE

Before we describe specific devices, be aware of your most powerful weapon—your mind. There's a time-tested fighting axiom that says, "Match the tactics to the situation." In threatening situations, no two scenarios are exactly the same, so tactics must be adjusted according to the circumstances of the attack. Then you must have the courage to put your tactics into action.

THE TUTOR

Marie was fascinated by her French heritage. After graduating from college, she moved to Paris and decided to begin her adventure by making money as an English tutor. She ran a small newspaper ad and soon had students coming to her apartment for English lessons.

One afternoon a young Frenchman showed up for a lesson. Soon after she let him in, her instincts told her she was in danger. As she tried to get him to leave, he grabbed her and threw her onto the sofa. She resisted, but he was too strong, and she realized he was going to rape her. Her mind raced for a solution. As he was removing her clothes, she said she would cooperate rather than be hurt. But she said she needed to get to the bathroom very quickly or she was going to make a big, unpleasant mess. He was reluctant, but she was persuasive. As soon as she was several steps away from him, she raced to her apartment door, opened it, screamed for help, and ran. He panicked and fled.

I hadn't heard about the, "I'm going to s---- all over us" tactic before this young woman shared it in one of our classes, but she used it effectively, and it saved her from being raped or worse.

Though many of the weapons and tactics we discuss will work in many scenarios, the "match the tactics to the situation" guideline is worth remembering. There is no more powerful and flexible weapon than your mind if you have time to use it, and, depending on the situation, you may devise creative tactics that will work effectively.

Devising alternative tactics, however, is restricted to timeframes before and after an attacker is physically trying to abduct you. If someone is trying to capture you, the cat move and other fighting actions must be immediate—reflexive. When facing abduction, focus on the overriding rule: do not get captured! Do not get transported! Do not give up!

WEAPON: STUFF YOU HAVE IN YOUR HANDS

If you are carrying a purse, laptop, gift packages, books, or any other objects with significant mass, they can be effective weapons.

AT THE MALL

Katie was shopping for her daughter's school clothes on a warm August afternoon. She had her purse and was focused on balancing several packages as she walked to her car in an upscale mall's parking lot.

As she juggled the packages and opened her car door, a man grabbed her arm and started pushing her into the car. Katie screamed as she threw the packages into his face. Then she started swinging her purse at him with all her might as she continued screaming at the top of her lungs. The man stopped pushing her and ran away.

Katie threw her packages at the attacker and screamed to disorient him. She followed up with more screams and blows from her purse. Though none of these were lethal threats, the attacker felt sufficiently surprised and the presence of sufficient resistance to stop his assault. Katie wasn't the victim for whom he was looking.

WEAPON: COMB/BRUSH, STICK, OR ANY OTHER RIGID, ABRASIVE OBJECT

A stiff comb, brush, stick, or any other rigid and abrasive object can be raked across an attacker's eyes. Though these devices are not particularly intimidating, having a brush in your hand as you walk to your car is better than having nothing if you need to face an attacker and convince him you are not going to be an easy victim.

PLUSES: Easy to carry, easy to use.

MINUSES: Not very intimidating; must be used at close range.

WEAPON: PENS AND KEYS

A pen, pencil, or any writing instrument with a sharp end and a rounded end is a modestly effective self-defense weapon. You almost always have a pen with you. Place the rounded end in the palm of your hand and extend the pointed end between your longest finger and ring finger as shown in the picture. If an attacker approaches, jab the pen toward his face while you make eye contact and retreat. If he pauses, continue your escape. If he attacks, use the pen in the same way you would use your fingers in a cat move.

Keys are better than nothing, but they're not very intimidating or effective except when used in combination with your strong attitude and eyes that say you won't submit. In this scenario, they reinforce your "I am not a victim" statement, but don't count on them to stop an attacker.

PLUSES: Easy to carry; easy to use; modest effectiveness.

MINUSES: Only modestly intimidating and must be used at close range.

WEAPON: **BATON**

Batons come in various lengths and weights. They are telescoping metal rods contained in a base rod that has a soft rubber cover. By vigorously flipping your wrist (similar to a Frisbee throwing motion), you can extend the rod segments, and they automatically lock in place, creating a solid rod.

Batons are easy to carry. Because they come in various sizes, you can pick a size that feels right and fits into your purse or pocket.

To use the baton, flick your wrist to extend it and then strike with a back-and-forth swinging motion.

PLUSES: Easy to carry; easy to use; modestly intimidating.

MINUSES: Only modestly intimidating and must be used at close range.

WEAPON: TASERS WITH SHOOTING ELECTRODES

 TASERS COME IN TWO FORMS: Those that shoot electrodes and those that do not.

Tasers with shooting electrodes are activated when you pull a trigger. The electrodes fly out to about 15' on the end of wires. When the two electrodes hit the attacker's skin, a strong electrical current flows through the attacker, causing pain and temporary paralysis. If you hit the attacker, you will effectively stop him. If you miss him, the device is useless. These devices cost several hundred dollars and are battery powered.

If you face a threatening situation, get the taser in your hand so you can react quickly if necessary. When an attacker approaches, aim the taser at him, make eye contact so he knows you are serious, and retreat. If he attacks, shoot him at close range (so you don't miss).

PLUSES: Easy to carry; quite intimidating; effective immobilizer.

MINUSES: You must hit the attacker when you shoot or the device becomes useless; there is danger to children, so you must control access to the device.

WEAPON: TASERS WITHOUT SHOOTING ELECTRODES

Tasers that do not shoot electrodes are typically about the size of a cigarette pack. They have two electrodes on one end and an activating button. These devices can be used for intimidation or immobilization. For intimidation (especially in low light conditions), you can push the activating button and a spark will jump across a gap between the electrodes. The spark is very bright and produces a crackling sound that is intimidating. For immobilization, you must press the electrodes against the attacker and push the button. The current will flow through a layer of normal clothing, but will not flow through heavy clothing or multiple layers of moderately thick material. Current flowing between the electrodes will produce pain and temporary paralysis. These devices have prices from about $50 to $150 and are battery powered.

PLUSES: Easy to carry; easy to use; fairly intimidating; effective immobilizer.

MINUSES: Some danger to children and must be used at close range.

WEAPON: SPRAYS

Sprays are available in various dispensers. All sprays are effective if you get them into the attacker's eyes or nose. Sprays are less intimidating than other weapons, but they are better than nothing when you are convincing an attacker that you are not a victim. If there is a breeze, you must be certain the spray disperses into the attacker's face and not yours.

PLUSES: Easy to carry; easy to use; effective when in the attacker's eyes and nose.

MINUSES: Modestly intimidating; risk that the chemicals may blow into your eyes; must be used at close range.

WEAPON: KNIVES

Knives come in many sizes and shapes. From the small slow-to-open common jackknife to fast-opening, spring-loaded weapons, these devices range from modestly intimidating to very intimidating. Though no one wants to be in a knife fight, a knife can be effective when you are communicating that you won't be a victim while you are retreating. By showing the knife, making aggressive eye contact, and holding the knife between you and the attacker as you retreat, you are making a strong statement that will dissuade many attackers. If, however, the attacker chases you and overcomes you, the knife can be used against you. Most women worry about losing the knife to the attacker and choose not to rely on a knife as their weapon of choice.

PLUSES: Easy to carry; easy to use; intimidating.

MINUSES: Must be used at close range; high fear factor related to the knife being turned on the victim.

THE WEAPONS WE HAVE DESCRIBED UP TO THIS POINT ARE AVAILABLE AT MANY FULL-SERVICE GUN SHOPS, AND YOU USUALLY NEED NO SPECIAL PERMITS OR TRAINING TO OWN THEM. IF YOU SPEND A LITTLE TIME SEARCHING THE INTERNET IN CATEGORIES RELATED TO WOMEN'S SELF-DEFENSE, YOU WILL FIND MANY SITES SELLING SELF-PROTECTION DEVICES.

WEAPON: GUNS

In life-and-death scenarios, serious combatants (police and soldiers) use the most effective self-defense devices currently available—guns. From an intimidation perspective, nothing works better. A woman with a gun can stop several attackers as she escapes. Remember that a pistol doesn't need to be fired in order to stop about 90% of all attackers. Beyond that, firing a pistol without killing the attacker prevents many additional assaults. Instances where a woman fires at an attacker and kills or seriously injures him are rare. The number is small enough that I have not been able to find reliable information to cite. So, as you consider whether to use a pistol or not, do not assume you must shoot someone to use this device effectively. In most cases, women use pistols to stop attackers without firing the weapon or seriously injuring the assailant.

PISTOL PACKING BLONDE

Tammy was an attractive blond and a businesswoman who had to be out after dark frequently. Her husband traveled often, so she became self-reliant. As part of her self-reliance, she learned to shoot a pistol, had a permit to carry, and carried a pistol in her fanny pack when she was out alone at night.

One evening she was walking home and noticed a man approaching on the opposite side of the street. After they passed each other, he came across the street and started to follow her. She walked faster. So did he. He was closing the distance between them. She reached into her fanny pack and got the pistol in her hand.

Then he started running to catch her. She ran for a short distance and decided that he was faster than she was and he was going to catch her. She turned and yelled, "Stop!" He kept coming.

She fired a shot into the ground between them. He was startled and stopped. She turned and ran toward a convenience store about half a block away. He walked after her. She went into the store and had the clerk call 911. He waited outside across the street.

When the police arrived and detained the man, they discovered he was under the influence of drugs. When they took him downtown, they found that he had a record of prior assaults.

Though showing a pistol to stop an attacker is the most common use of this device and actually firing a pistol at an attacker is a rare occurrence, you must understand and accept that shooting the weapon at an attacker is a possibility. If you choose to defend yourself with a pistol, you must get proper training. To do that, go to a credible training facility, such as an established gun store or a self-defense pistol specialist. If you have no prior training, you may be surprised how easy it is to become adequately proficient with a pistol. Most women find that once they get over their initial fear, shooting guns is fun and practice is enjoyable.

WOMEN ARE THE FASTEST GROWING GROUP OF NEW SHOOTERS IN SHOOTING SPORTS

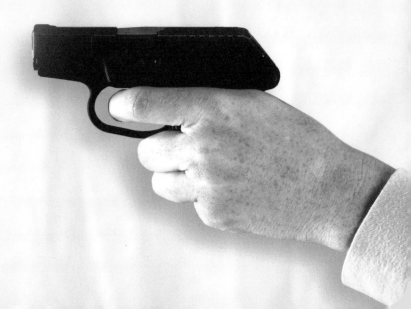

If you decide to use a pistol, you must manage the risk to those around you. This is critically important, but it is easier than you may imagine. When you receive gun training, talk to the instructor about your particular circumstances and create a safe-storage plan. Millions of people successfully do this. Safe storage is very important, but not difficult. In our home the self-defense pistol in our bedroom is in a small gun safe designed to protect the pistol until my wife or I need it to stop an intruder. Details regarding using a pistol to defend yourself at home are in a later chapter.

PLUSES: The most effective intimidation device; the most effective stopping device.

MINUSES: Training required for safe handling and use; safe storage is necessary; a permit may be required for use outside your home.

CELL PHONES

Cell phones aren't weapons. Talking on a cell phone compromises your hearing and your ability to focus. When you are facing danger, your Threat Alarm needs all the input it can get. Use your cell phone before or after, but not during, a time when you sense danger.

Prepare

SELECT A WEAPON YOU ARE COMFORTABLE USING.

PRACTICE WITH IT AND CARRY IT. IF YOU MUST FIGHT,

USE YOUR WEAPON WITH SURPRISE AND VIOLENT FORCE

SO YOU CAN ESCAPE AS THE ATTACKER DEALS WITH PAIN.

chapter 5

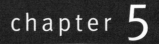

The Twilight
Zone

The Twilight Zone

REMEMBER:

About 70% of assaults happen after dark. 60%–70% of assaults involve alcohol or drugs.

Remember: About 70% of assaults happen after dark. 60%–70% of assaults involve alcohol or drugs. Other than in and around homes, locations around cars are the most dangerous.

This chapter covers precautions for high risk situations. We'll start with darkness, alcohol, and drugs. They are part of the twilight zone—it's a dangerous place.

SITUATION 1.
"GIRLS JUST WANNA HAVE FUN."

DARK + ALCOHOL/DRUGS =
HIGH RISK

About 80% of assaults occur from age 12 to 34. These are party years when girls/women are learning about men, alcohol, and drugs.

THE PARTY I DON'T REMEMBER

Three girlfriends went out on Saturday night. It was time to have some fun. They went to a popular bar, and the place was rockin'. After a few drinks, they were on a roll—joking, laughing, and flirting.

POSSIBLE OUTCOME 1: About 10 o'clock, Terri lost track of what was happening. Her girlfriends realized she was drunk and stayed with her. They continued having fun until they all went home together at closing time. The next day Terri couldn't remember much, and her friends had to tell her what happened.

POSSIBLE OUTCOME 2: About 10 o'clock Terri, lost track of what was happening. She met a fun guy. Her girlfriends said she should stay with them, but she was having fun dancing with him. Eventually the girlfriends decided it was time to leave, and they tried to get Terri to go with them. She said that she could take care of herself, and they should let her have fun. The girlfriends gave up and left Terri with the guy. The next morning Terri woke up in a hotel room and knew something was very wrong. She was naked, and she knew that she had had sex. What she didn't know was with whom. Humiliated, scared, and not knowing what to say if the police asked her questions, she didn't report what happened. But she lived in fear of pregnancy and STDs until tests told her she was going to be okay.

STUDYING TOGETHER

Jenny lived in an affluent suburb where kids had access to money and prescription drugs their parents used. Even though her middle school friends experimented with pills, she didn't.

One Saturday, a couple boys from school called her and said they were going to study together and asked if she wanted to come over. She thought it would be fun, so she joined them. As they talked, one of the boys asked her if she wanted a Coke. She said yes, and he got her the drink. Shortly thereafter, everything went blurry.

She woke up in a hospital. The doctors told her parents that apparently the boys had drugged Jenny and then spent time putting things inside her. At some point, she began to bleed, and the boys called 911. These fourteen year-old boys had torn up Jenny so badly that the doctors feared it may affect her ability to have children.

As you think about "having fun," include the following in your plans:

- Don't party alone. If you party without friends, you become easy prey for a predator. Go with a trustworthy friend or group of friends.

AGREE TO THREE SIMPLE RULES:

- **STRANGERS—NO GO.** None of you will leave alone with a stranger.

- **TOO DRUNK—NO GO.** If one of you gets drunk, the others will not allow that girl to leave with any male, including friends.

- **DRUGS—WE ALL GO.** If someone in your group appears drugged, you will all leave together immediately.

If someone you don't trust completely buys you a drink and you don't see the drink all the way from the bartender's hands to you, don't drink it. Sometimes that's not even enough to remain safe.

DOUBLE TEAMED

Tania and Angie were new in town, and they went to visit a neighborhood bar. It seemed like a friendly place. Many of the guys were regulars, and everyone knew the bartenders.

Tania met a guy, and they started joking around and having fun. He seemed nice. She spent most of the evening talking with him.

Just before closing time, Angie could see that Tania was disoriented, even though she continued talking with the guy. He was trying to get her to go to a party at his place after the bar closed. Tania was sounding like she wanted to go. Angie intervened. Even though Tania wanted to go, and the guy was getting really irritated with Angie's interference, Angie took control and got Tania back to their car. They went home. The next morning Tania didn't remember the end of the evening.

A month later the word was out that one of bartenders and the guy had been picked up by police for drugging a girl and using her at a "private party" after the bar closed. The bartender was a close friend of the guy, and he put drugs in the girl's drink for his buddy. When the guy got the girl to his place, the bartender joined the party. The girl woke up in her car the next morning and couldn't remember what had happened. She was sore and knew she had been raped.

Though she was embarrassed, she went straight to the police, told them what she could remember, and went through an examination. Evidence was found. Police used what she had told them, plus information from a similar case that happened at the same bar, and caught the two.

In almost every "Not Me!" class I teach, one or more women share tragic stories about how men used party-related drugs or alcohol to take advantage of girls and women. A large percentage of these assaults are not reported because the victims are too embarrassed. As a result, the victims do not get help and the bad guys get away with their crime. "Girls having fun" can be much safer if they make simple commitments to one another and then honor them. Figure out the rules you want to use and follow them. If one of the women in your group gets carried away and wants to break the rules, get her home. That's what friends do for friends.

IF LOOKS COULD KILL...

Ed Gein, Richard Speck, Ted Bundy, Jeffrey Dahmer, Clifford Olsen, and John Wayne Gacy.... All of these men were serial killers, and all of them looked perfectly normal. You can't tell what's inside a man by looking at the surface.

JUST BECAUSE A BOY OR MAN LOOKS NORMAL, THAT TELLS YOU NOTHING ABOUT HOW HE MAY ACT IF HE HAS YOU ISOLATED.

THIS MAN IS A CONVICTED MURDERER.

Your Threat Alarm is a reliable, but quiet, signal. Unless you pause and actually ask your Threat Alarm to give you a reading on someone, you may be so preoccupied that its warning signal gets lost in the static of your activity. I don't know how to avoid this problem because all of us who are guilty of enthusiasm are susceptible to overpowering or over-thinking our protecting signal. Busy-ness can simply overwhelm a subtle Threat Alarm signal until it's too late and you are isolated and being attacked.

The best way to avoid being trapped by a man who looks normal is to avoid letting any man isolate you unless you totally trust him. Before you separate from a group, ask your Threat Alarm if the man is a threat. Listen to the response. If you feel any pause or hesitation, no matter how slight, do not become isolated with the man even though you may know him well.

SITUATION 2. GETTING AROUND.

EYE CONTACT AND POSTURE

Predators assess eye contact and posture as they interview women. The predator will rank potential victims on a scale from "not vulnerable" to "quite vulnerable." A characteristic of vulnerable women is that they tend to avoid eye contact and have submissive postures. The most vulnerable women actively avoid eye contact and appear very submissive in the presence of an assertive person. Predators are interviewing you; don't give them reason to pursue you.

YOU'RE NOT GETTIN' ANY

A group of girls had been having dinner at a nice restaurant. During dinner, they noticed a man sitting at the bar who was staring at them. It made them uncomfortable, but they just ignored it and tried to laugh it off. After dinner, they decided to move to another bar down the street.

They ordered their drinks and settled in a booth in the corner. Then one of the girls spotted the man from the restaurant. He had followed them there, and he continued with his awkward stare. But the girls weren't having it. One of them stood up, walked straight over to him, looked him in the eye, and said loudly, "What the hell do you think you're doing? We saw you at the restaurant. Stop with the staring and stop with the following. You're not gettin' any."

The man looked around the bar to see who had heard this. Many people had. He stood up without a word and left the bar in a hurry.

ON THE BUS

Kristin rode the bus and took the subway frequently. It was the easiest way to get around her busy city. She was accustomed to crowded situations where casual contact was unavoidable, but this guy was going too far.

At every bump and turn his hands were on her hips. She glared at him, but he didn't stop. It got worse. Finally, she looked him in the eye and yelled, "Get your damn hands off me!" He was embarrassed and moved away from her. Men near her kept a respectful distance while other women made eye contact with Kristin, quietly nodding their approval.

To avoid becoming a target because you look like a victim, do the following:

> When making eye contact, treat the person you are looking at just as you would any other presence in your immediate area. Look at the person, recognize him, and then move on. Do not avoid eye contact. Treat the person just as you would a new car or building that you just recognized. Look at it and then move on.

> If a person challenges you with their eyes by staring at you, look at them, recognize their presence, and then look away as you move away. The intimidator's challenging look will have tripped your Threat Alarm. You know that as soon as your Threat Alarm goes off, your immediate response is to move away…get space between you and the threat. You are in Yellow moving away from a possible threat. If the person pursues you, move away strongly and go into Red.

ATMs

You are vulnerable when you face an ATM with your attention focused on the machine and your back exposed. Minimize the time you spend facing the ATM. To be safer, get your card and numbers ready before you reach the machine. Insert your card and enter your numbers. Then turn and put your back to the machine as you wait for the transaction to be completed. When you are ready to complete the transaction, turn back to the machine just long enough to retrieve your money and card. Minimize time with your back exposed to potential threats.

SUBWAYS, TRAINS, BUSES

Ride near the operator or driver. Ride in a car with more people rather than fewer people. Don't get isolated with one man or a small group of men with whom you are uncomfortable. If you are about to be isolated with one man or a small group of men, trust your Threat Alarm. If it gives you any danger signal, get off and figure out a safe way to proceed.

MUGGING

If a mugger confronts you and demands your wallet, purse, or other valuable items, you must make an instant decision. Experienced people agree that it is best to give up your valuables and protect your body. Rehearse this in your mind: toss your valuables in one direction and then run in the opposite direction. Make the mugger choose between your valuables and you. If all he wants is the valuables, he will move toward them as you escape.

**DO NOT HAND YOUR VALUABLES TO THE MUGGER.
IF HE TOUCHES YOU, HE MAY DECIDE TO ESCALATE FROM
THEFT TO AN ASSAULT ON YOU.**

SITUATION 3. AROUND CARS.

KEEP YOUR CAR DOORS LOCKED WHEN PARKED AND DRIVING

Locked doors keep predators out, whether you are in your car or not. The only time your car doors should be unlocked is when you are getting in or out. Once you get in or out, lock the doors again immediately.

THE STALKER

Kit and her girlfriend were enjoying the house they rented as both of them jumped into their new jobs. Life was good —except for the guy across the street.

Initially, Kit had politely said "Hi" to him several times. It seemed like the neighborly thing to do. But now he was either watching her from his windows or his yard whenever she was around her house. It didn't feel right.

One day he stood in his yard watching her as she worked in her garden. She asked him if he would please stop looking at her, but he ignored her request. Uncomfortable, she went indoors and started avoiding time in her front yard. Soon she felt that enough was enough, and she called the police, complaining that she felt he was stalking her. The police asked some questions, but finally said that up to that point he had broken no laws and there was nothing they could do. They said she should call them if he came onto her property or tried to get close to her.

A week later, Kit was leaving for work in the morning as usual. She went into her garage, switched on the light, and opened her car door. As was her usual practice, she glanced into the backseat. There, on the floor, was the guy from across the street, trying to hide. Kate screamed, slammed the car door, ran back into her house, locked the door, and called 911. This time the police had enough to arrest the guy.

LOOK IN THE BACKSEAT SPACE BEFORE YOU GET INTO YOUR CAR

And have a strong light in your garage so that you can see into the backseat clearly.

WALK FACING THE TRAFFIC, NOT WITH THE TRAFFIC

If you walk with the traffic (the traffic is approaching you from behind), a car can approach you and slow down without you seeing it. As it comes alongside you, an attacker can get out of the passenger side, grab you by surprise, and force you into the car. If you walk facing the traffic, you'll be able to see a car slow down, see a potential attacker looking at you, see the door open, and see him coming at you. At some point in that sequence, your Threat Alarm will go off and you can immediately react by running away and screaming.

DON'T LET ANYONE INTO YOUR CAR UNLESS YOU TRUST THE PERSON TOTALLY

There are thousands of stories about well-intentioned women who have reluctantly given rides to men who supposedly needed a lift. Somewhere along the way these men have used intimidation, "Cooperate or I'll kill you," or weapons to get the woman to an isolated place. Once isolated, the men attacked the women. These women had to make a critical choice:

CHOICE A: Create a reason why you can't give the man a ride, even though doing so may be embarrassing.

CHOICE B: Give the man a ride and potentially face torture, rape, or death.

Rely on your Threat Alarm. If you feel any discomfort whatsoever, don't become isolated in the car with a man.

STAY IN YOUR CAR UNLESS YOU FEEL SAFE

BAD VIBES

What a great time she'd had at the party. Pat was wishing she could have stayed, but it was late, and she had a full day planned for tomorrow. As she drove through the quiet suburbs, her mind was imagining how much fun she and her friends would have at the beach. She pulled up to the stop sign and noticed headlights approaching from the rear. "It's not slowing down enough! Noooo!" Crunch.

Why didn't that car slow down enough? The impact wasn't very hard, but there might be damage.

A guy is getting out of the car. It's dark.

This doesn't feel right.

Pat made sure her doors were locked and rolled her window down about an inch. Her car was still running. The guy seemed normal, but the situation didn't feel right. They were too isolated.

"I'll drive up to the gas station so we can see our cars under the light," Pat said.

"We can do it here," he said.

"No, let's go to the gas station," she responded. And then she slowly accelerated, heading to the gas station several blocks ahead.

As she looked into the rearview mirror, she saw the man's car turn right and drive away. *Weird.*

The next day she learned that a woman had been assaulted after stopping for a minor traffic accident on a side street near her incident.

IF SOMEONE TRIES TO BREAK INTO YOUR CAR, USE YOUR ACCELERATOR TO ESCAPE

AT THE STOPLIGHT

Cathy had to work a little late. It was dusk as she began her drive home. The light that always seemed to be red got her again. As she sat waiting for the light to turn green, a man ran from the building on the corner and jumped in front of her car, putting his hands on its hood. At the same time, another man ran from the building and started opening the passenger side door.

In a fraction of a second, Cathy felt disbelief, shock, and overwhelming fear. She froze. If she tried to drive the car away, she would have to go over the man with his

hands on her hood. But the other man was opening the passenger door.

Her choices were clear: remain stopped and face the man coming through the passenger door or accelerate into the man in front of her car. In an instant she decided she was not going to be a victim, and she pressed evenly on the accelerator. The man in front felt the car move and pushed himself away while the man in the passenger door lost his footing and grabbed the door for support. As she cleared the man in front, Cathy accelerated and the man in the passenger door fell as he lost his grip. She watched her attackers staggering on the pavement in her rearview mirror as she drove to safety.

There are hundreds of horsepower under your right foot. Use that power to get away from trouble.

CRASH RATHER THAN GET ISOLATED

If an attacker is transporting you, one of you is driving. If you are driving, pick a location near other vehicles and people, then crash your car into a tree, post, building, or anything else that will stop the vehicle. If the attacker is driving, look for a time when he is focused on traffic or turning and then grab the wheel with all your might, forcing him to lose control and crash into something solid.

IS IT DIFFICULT TO CHOOSE CRASHING?

CHOICE A: Crash the car and risk injury from the collision.

CHOICE B: Don't crash the car, get isolated, and suffer torture, rape, or death.

GIVEN THAT 90% OF STRANGER ABDUCTIONS RESULT IN TERRIBLE CONSEQUENCES, THE DECISION DOESN'T SEEM DIFFICULT

NOT ALL PEOPLE WHO WEAR UNIFORMS ARE TRUSTWORTHY POLICE OFFICERS

Nearly every police officer is a good person, willing to put his/her life on the line for your safety. But there are exceptions and impostors. If you are pulled over by a person wearing a uniform in a place where you don't feel safe, protect yourself using any of the following tactics:

- Do not get out of your car except in a public, lighted, safe place.

- If you see police car lights behind you and you are in an unsafe area, slow down to well under the speed limit so he knows you are aware of his presence and keep rolling until you are at a safe place.

- If you are not in a public, lighted, safe area, dial 911 and report your location to police as you keep rolling slowly. Ask them to confirm that a police officer is making the stop. Leave the line open until the stop is completed.

- If you pull over to the side of the road, keep your car engine running and roll your window down about an inch. Tell the officer that you want to cooperate, but you want to move slowly to a more public, lighted place. If the officer understands and will allow you to do so, then proceed. If the officer tries to stop you from moving to a more public, lighted place, press the accelerator and get away from him at a safe speed. Proceed to the nearest safe place and stop there.

- If you have On Star or a similar service, open the line and report what is happening if your Threat Alarm tells you anything is not right.

- When in doubt, keep rolling at a slow, safe speed until you are in a safe place.

Let the situation dictate the tactics you choose, but don't allow yourself to become a victim simply because a man is wearing a uniform. You may have to explain your actions to the officer or to a court, but this is an acceptable problem given the alternative of possible abduction in a dark secluded place. Legitimate law officers and judges in courts will understand what you have done so long as you proceed slowly and safely from the stop site to the nearest safe place.

DON'T STOP IN AN UNSAFE PLACE FOR A FLAT TIRE OR MINOR MECHANICAL PROBLEM

We all know that driving on a flat tire can damage that tire beyond repair. It's a good idea not to drive on a low or flat tire. However, if you have a tire problem and you are in an unsafe place, continue driving until you reach a safe place. It may be a bumpy ride, but your car will get you there. Better to damage a tire and remain safe than stop in a risky place.

If another motorist flashes lights or waves at you, indicating a problem with your car, and you are in an area that feels unsafe, do not stop. If your car is drivable, continue moving until you reach an area that is safe before you stop to determine what the other driver was trying to communicate.

THE PANIC BUTTON ON YOUR KEY RING IS VALUABLE

Any time you are threatened near your car, push the panic button. If you choose to carry no weapon, at least have a finger on your panic button when you go to or from your car. Should an attacker appear, push the button and the alarm will surprise him, creating your opportunity to escape.

Your key ring panic button can also be valuable at home if your car is close by. Should an attacker enter your home, push the button sounding your car alarm. Try your panic button at home to see if it works. You want to keep your key ring in your bedroom at night.

Prepare

USE THE SAFETY GUIDELINES ABOVE AND CREATE

MORE OF YOUR OWN.

chapter

Cyber
Safety

chapter 6

Cyber Safety

C U LOL

We all have wants and needs—to be popular, to be recognized, to be attractive, to have things. There is a place you can get all this. It's a place where you can be who you want to be and no one can put you down. It's the Internet. And it's easy to get there because you have to be online. Schools require it for homework. Your friends communicate that way. It's where you get answers to questions. It's many good things. But it can be dangerous if you don't understand that predators use it to interview and connect with victims.

Dangerous people monitor the sites you visit and groups with whom you chat. Your Internet communications expose who you are and what you want. Predators are skilled at interpreting this information, and they can use it to connect with you and persuade you that they are someone you want to meet. Then they isolate you so they can attack. Does this seem like a stretch? It's not at all.

I have seen real cases where a bad guy took an innocent email from a teenage girl and moved from one search engine to another, one website to another, gathering the following information in less than twenty minutes:

Her name, address, and telephone number.

Her parents' names, jobs, and phone numbers.

Her siblings' names.

Her school and its location.

Her best friends' names.

Her favorite activities or sports.

Directions to her home and an image of her yard and neighborhood.

Likely times when she will be home alone.

Twenty minutes is all he needed to gather this information. Given more time, he found out more. With all this information, he created his plan to connect with her and isolate her.

YOUNG GIRLS ARE NOT THE ONLY TARGETS.

MATURE WOMEN ARE VULNERABLE ALSO.

INTERNET FRAUD

Heather met a man through an online social network. They had been chatting and exchanging emails for a couple weeks, and she already felt as though she knew him. They talked about their lives, their dreams, their insecurities. He was surprisingly open with every aspect of his life. He was kind and understanding, and he always gave great advice. He seemed like the perfect man. Not to mention, he was drop-dead gorgeous. All of the pictures he had on his site portrayed him as a fun, handsome guy whom everyone loved. Heather was excited.

They decided to meet at a local bar. They had a couple drinks, and he was just as charming in person as he was in writing. Heather couldn't believe her luck. After a couple more drinks, he suggested they go to another bar, his favorite haunt. They decided to take her car, because parking at this other place was difficult and parking one car would be easier than two.

As they drove, Heather started to feel a little dizzy. Next thing she knew, she woke up to frantic knocking on her window. She was undressed and in the passenger seat of her car. There was blood on her face and hands. She didn't know if it was hers. Heather looked outside the window, and to her surprise it was the next morning.

He had taken advantage of her and then left her in her car on the side of the road. After talking to police, she went back to his page on the social network. It was gone. And he seemed like the perfect man.

Using information gathered from various Internet sources, predators create the reality you want. They become your friend, confidant, adviser, or lover. They make themselves seem perfect because they have worked to learn important things about you. Once you trust them, they can hurt you and disappear as fast as it takes to hit "Delete."

We all have fantasies or dreams we want to realize. The Internet makes it easy to immerse ourselves in Second Lives, MySpace, or other fantasy realities. There is nothing wrong with healthy joys and satisfactions we grant ourselves in these entertaining cyber pastimes. But understand that fantasy is fantasy, and reality is different. In fantasy, things can be too good to be true, and there are no consequences. In reality, if things are too good to be true, they probably are too good to be true.

Good things can come from cyber connections, but the guys who step out of the Internet are not men you know. Use common sense. Ask your Threat Alarm about men from the Internet. If you get a negative feeling or even a slight hesitation, then don't get isolated with a man until you have spent enough time with him in the real world to know who he really is.

Prepare

CREATE INTERNET RELATIONSHIPS WITH THE SAME

DISCRETION YOU USE ON THE STREET.

chapter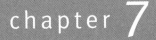

Safer at
Home

chapter 7

Safer at Home

REMEMBER:

Over half of all assaults happen in or around your home or the homes of relatives/ friends/ neighbors.

REMEMBER: Over half of all assaults happen in or around your home or the home of a relative/ friend/neighbor.

Though home is nearly always a very safe place (la-la land White), prepare yourself for those times when intruders can turn it into a Black place.

Intruders are very dangerous. A thief will enter your home when you are not there because he wants your stuff, not you. But intruders who enter your house while you're there may want contact with you. In the isolation of your home, very bad things can happen.

There are several simple actions that will make your home safer. You have probably heard the terms "hard" and "soft" targets. Hard targets are those that are prepared to deal with a threat; soft targets are those that are not well prepared. Select any or all of the following actions to increase intruders' perception that your home is a hard target.

PUT A SECURITY COMPANY SIGN BY YOUR DRIVEWAY AND SECURITY COMPANY DECALS ON THE MAIN DOORS

Whether you have a security system or not, the sign and decals will encourage potential intruders to look for a victim somewhere else that does not have a security system.

PUT A "BEWARE OF DOG" SIGN IN A VISIBLE PLACE

Whether you have a dog or not, intruders would rather not worry about the problem and will likely move on to a place without dogs.

PUT A MOTION-ACTIVATED SECURITY LIGHT ABOVE YOUR FRONT AND BACK DOORS

These lights are not expensive and are fairly easy to install. They turn your lights on when there is motion in the area around your doors. If an intruder is selecting a target, he would prefer one where he is not going to be performing center stage under a bright light.

LOCK ALL YOUR DOORS AND WINDOWS

Even though a locked door or window may not stop a determined intruder, the noise created by his breaking a lock will give you warning so you can call 911 and prepare for what's happening.

If, despite your precautionary actions, an intruder enters your home, the time to choose an action plan is now, before that scary time comes. Just as you have prepared yourself and your children for dealing with a fire in your home, prepare for the possibility that you may have an intruder. When you prepare for the possibility of a fire, you remember simple rules for when the smoke alarm goes off. If you are in your bedroom and the door feels hot, don't open it. If smoke is coming under the door, don't go out there. The escape plan may be to open the bedroom window and crawl outside or jump onto the lawn below. These actions are unpleasant to think about, but you have a plan, and your loved ones know what to do.

Do the same thing for a night intruder. Have a plan so everyone knows what to do.

There are three general plans for dealing with an intruder. Choice 1 is victim behavior. Choice 2 is mildly proactive. Choice 3 is "Not me!" behavior.

CHOICE 1. **HIDE-AND-HOPE.** Using this strategy, you get under the bed, go into the closet, or get out of sight, hoping that the intruder just wants your stuff. If the intruder is just a thief and doesn't find you while he's stealing, this strategy can work. If, however, he is there because he wants to hurt you, or if he finds you while he is stealing and sees an opportunity to hurt you as well as steal, then the hide-and-hope strategy is not effective. Hide-and-hope is victim behavior because it gives too much control to the attacker.

CHOICE 2. **ESCAPE.** Using this strategy, you intend to get out of the house, hoping the intruder does not catch you or chase you. If you or your children have bedrooms on the first floor, this strategy can work. If your bedrooms are on the second or third stories, this strategy is dangerous. Though choosing Escape is more proactive than Hide-and-Hope, it still gives the intruder control and forces you to simply react.

CHOICE 3. PREPARE-AND-RESIST. This is the "Not me!" strategy. Prepare by having a family meeting where you discuss what the family will do if an intruder comes to your home (you can simultaneously review the rules about not getting in any car with strangers and what to do if the smoke alarm goes off). If anyone hears an intruder breaking a window or door lock, everyone immediately goes to Mom and Dad's bedroom (the safe room). If children sleep on a different floor, they lock their bedroom door or go to a safe room with a door lock, such as the bathroom, and lock the door until Mom or Dad come to get them. As soon as the children have gone to the safe room, they call 911 for help. This is all the children need to know. They do not need to know what follows below.

gun safe in headboard or drawer

What the parents know is that in their bedroom are three things: phone, pistol, and tac light (tactical light—that's a fancy name for a flashlight that has an activating switch on its end rather than on its side). The pistol and tac light are safely stored in a small gun safe near the bed. Once the children are in the master bedroom, everyone gets together behind some cover, such as a bed. One of you calls 911 to get help while the other holds the pistol and the tac light.

If the intruder is just taking things and is not coming near the bedroom, everyone stays quiet except for the person talking in a low voice to the 911 operator. If the intruder starts coming upstairs or down the hall to the bedroom, then the person with the pistol and the light yells, "Get out of here! We are talking with 911, and the police are coming right now! Don't come in here!" Hopefully the intruder will become scared and leave. But if he is drunk, on drugs, or has been stalking you, he may continue coming toward your bedroom. You must decide what to do when you see him in the doorway. To help your decision, remember that:

HE BROKE INTO YOUR HOME
He has no regard for the law or the sanctity of your home.

HE HAD AN OPPORTUNITY TO JUST TAKE STUFF AND LEAVE
He is doing more than that; he apparently wants contact with you.

HE IGNORED YOUR WARNINGS AND IS COMING INTO YOUR BEDROOM
This is the most private place in your home, and he is invading it.

Law enforcement people have seen what happens to people when bad guys capture them in the isolation of their homes. The bad guys frequently separate and isolate the family members, rape/torture/abuse them individually, and then kill them so no witnesses survive.

In most states, the practical standard that dictates when you are justified using deadly force (a gun) is linked to whether or not a reasonable person would conclude that the intruder is about to commit a felony against a person. If a reasonable person would conclude that the intruder is about to assault a person in their home, then deadly force is justified. If you have done what is outlined above, a reasonable person knows that this person has broken into your home, ignored your instructions to get out of your house, and ignored your warnings that the police are coming. Now the intruder is coming into your bedroom.

GIVEN THIS SCENARIO, DEADLY FORCE IS PROBABLY JUSTIFIABLE.

You must decide what is right for you and your family. In our house, whoever has the tac light and pistol will illuminate the intruder as he comes through our bedroom doorway. It will be clear in an instant whether we know the person or not. If the person is someone we know and is drunk or under chemical influence and appears to be in our home by mistake, we will use restraint. If the person is someone we don't know, the intruder will be shot rather than allowed to enter our bedroom. If the intruder is shot, we will remain behind cover until the police arrive, because the intruder may have an accomplice and we don't want to become vulnerable to an attack by the accomplice while we are engaged with the first intruder.

When the police arrive, they will know what has been happening because of their contact with 911. 911 will tell you when the police have arrived at your home. Before the police get to your bedroom, put the pistol on the bed in front of you and hold your empty hands up to show police that you do not have a pistol. Then have your meltdown and let the police handle the situation.

If you use the Prepare-and-Resist strategy, you will have protected yourself and your loved ones. All your children have to know is:

- If you hear something that sounds like an intruder, come to our bedroom and tell us. If you hear us yell, "Intruder," come to our bedroom (or go to your safe room and lock the door).

- Then we'll call 911 and get help.

They don't need to know about other portions of the plan that may scare them.

So these are your three choices. Prepare-and-Resist is the most proactive. Escape is the intermediate choice. Hide-and-Hope is the most victim-like. If you are not comfortable with Prepare-and-Resist, then select Escape or Hide-and-Hope. But please don't live in denial. Any plan is better than no plan. Pick your plan and have your family meeting so everyone knows what to do if something bad happens.

Prepare

MAKE YOUR HOME APPEAR TO BE A HARD TARGET

COMPARED TO OTHERS. KNOW WHAT YOUR PLAN IS IF YOU

HAVE A NIGHT INTRUDER—BEFORE YOU HAVE ONE.

chapter 8

Living
Safer

chapter 8

Living Safer

KNOWLEDGE YIELDS POWER. Remember the quiz at the beginning of the book? Here are the answers.

Out of 100 women, how many are likely to be sexually assaulted during their lifetime? *Pick one.*

Fewer than 10 women _____

10 to 15 women _____

15 to 30 women <u> *x* </u>

Over 30 women _____

Which age groups suffer the most sexual assaults? Rank these choices from 1 (most assaults) to 5 (fewest assaults):

Age 13 to 19 <u> *1* </u>

Age 20 to 25 <u> *2* </u>

Age 26 to 32 <u> *3* </u>

Age 33 to 39 <u> *4* </u>

Age 40+ <u> *5* </u>

The woman will know the attacker in what percentage of assaults? *Pick one.*

Under 20% _____

25% to 50% _____

50% to 75% _____

75%+ ___*x*___

The male or female will have been drinking or using drugs in what percentage of assaults? *Pick one.*

Under 25% _____

25% to 50% _____

50%+ ___*x*___

What percentage of abductions by a stranger lead to assault, rape, or murder? *Pick one.*

50%+ _____

60%+ _____

70%+ _____

80%+ _____

90%+ ___*x*___

What percentage of assaults happen between dusk and dawn? *Pick one.*

Under 25% _____

25% to 50% _____

50% to 70% _____

70%+ ___*x*___

Of women who fought, what percentage believe that their resistance improved the outcome (made things better)? *Pick one.*

Under 25%   _____

25% to 50%   _____

50% to 75%   _____

Over 75%   _x____

Now you have information, and that information has power. You know when you are most at risk. You know who is most likely to attack you. You know how to recognize threatening situations. You know how to defend yourself.

Athletes, musicians, dancers, artists, trial lawyers—all great performers know the value of visualization. They see the setting, and they create their performance in their mind before it happens. These visualizations improve performance. You can do the same thing in order to be safer.

Using the information you now have, see yourself in la-la land White as you snuggle in your very safe place. See yourself transition into Yellow as you enjoy your day with your Threat Alarm turned on. See the times when you are most vulnerable—leaving your home, around your car early in the day, around your car late in the day, and at evening events. Imagine how you will react to the scenarios in this book if they become real in your life.

VISUALIZE WINNING. See a threat coming at you when you are in your car, and see the response that gets you away from the problem.

VISUALIZE WINNING. See someone trying to grab you from the front, the side, or the rear, and see yourself deciding "Not me!" as you use the cat move or other actions that let you escape from the attacker.

VISUALIZE WINNING. See how you are going to make your home safer, and see what you will do if you hear some unknown person in your home.

VISUALIZE WINNING. See yourself at a party and know the rules you will use to be safer.

Now see yourself enjoying life fully as you move through the day knowing that your Threat Alarm will give you warnings when you need them and your preparation will help keep you safer if a threat enters your space.

None of us can be safe all the time, but with what you've learned in this book and with visualizations of how you will handle threats, you will be safer.

YOU'LL PLAY THE WAY YOU PRACTICE. PRACTICE WINNING IN YOUR MIND.

And if you only remember one image from this book, let it be the one below.

YOU LOSE
IF YOU GIVE UP.
NEVER GIVE UP.
NEVER.

BLESS YOU. BE SAFER.

Appendix

Precautions

PREPARATION WHEN YOU TRAVEL:

Dress simply with no flashy jewelry that draws attention.

AT THE AIRPORT

- Arrange to be dropped off and picked up by someone you know.

- If you have to park, get close to an elevator or use valet service.

- If you have to walk any significant distance, get a security guard escort.

- On the airplane, don't give strangers information about where you are staying; don't let them see your itinerary and accommodations information.

WHEN YOU ARRIVE AT YOUR DESTINATION AIRPORT

- Have someone you know pick you up if possible.

- If you take a cab, do the following:

    - use cabs from the starter, no freelancers.

    - make certain that the picture on the cab permit matches the face of your driver.

- Know the route to your destination using MapQuest or equivalent.
- Have instructions written in the local language.

AT YOUR HOTEL

- Request a "women only" floor if the hotel has one.
- Get a room near the elevator so you don't have to wander long halls.
- If someone is threatening you, yell, "Fire!" to get more attention than "Help!"
- Check to make certain your room is safe before you deadbolt the door.
- Guard your room number so strangers can't determine where you are staying.
- Let no one into your room except uniformed room service people delivering items you ordered.

GETTING AROUND

- Get rides from people you know as much as possible.
- Use cabs from the hotel's starter rather than freelancers.
- Know where you are going and know the best route.
- Get written directions in the local language.
- Do not get out of the cab until you are at your destination; close is not good enough.

IF YOU GET INTO TROUBLE

- Know whom you are going to call if you get into trouble.
- Know if the local police are trustworthy.

- Know the number for the U.S. Consulate or other friendly resource if local officials are not trustworthy.

- Stay in Yellow. If something feels wrong, get away immediately.

PREPARATION AROUND HOME:

- Make your house appear to be a "hard target" by showing "Beware of dog" and "Security System" signs.

- Put up motion-activated lights by the front and back entrances.

- Replace or re-key locks when you move into a new home or apartment.

- Install good quality deadbolt door locks.

- Lock doors and windows—forcing intruders to make noise on the way in.

- Have a family meeting and agree on your intruder strategy—Hide-and-Hope, Escape, or Prepare-and-Resist.

- Open your door only for people you know and trust. Only let service or repair people in whom you have scheduled in advance.

- If you come home and see anything unusual, find someone you trust to enter the house with you or call 911.

- Do not let someone in to make a phone call—make the call for him.

- If someone enters your home, go into Yellow. If anything feels wrong, get away immediately.

PREPARATION AROUND CARS:

- Keep a map in your car to help you if you get lost.

- Lock your doors both when you are in your car and when it is parked.

- Allow only people you trust completely to be in your car with you.

- If you are being followed, drive to a police/fire station or a place where there are bright lights and many people.

- Have your car key detachable from your home key when giving your keys to a parking attendant or valet.

- Do not stop in an unsafe place. Drive to safety on flat tires and with minor damage to your car.

- Look in the backseat before you get into your car.

- If you have car trouble, raise your hood and stay in your locked vehicle. When someone offers help, roll your window down just a little to get help. Stay in your locked car until someone you trust arrives.

- If someone tries to force his way into your car, use the accelerator and escape.

- If an attacker is forcing you to drive to isolation, crash into something solid (tree, telephone pole, etc.) and escape.

- If an attacker is driving you to isolation, try to cause a crash into something solid and escape.

- Carry a cell phone to get help in emergencies.

- Stay in Yellow. If anything feels wrong, get away immediately.

PREPARATION ON THE STREET:

- Walk in groups; not alone.

- Walk around areas that can hide attackers (alleys, bushes).

- Avoid dark areas.

- Walk facing traffic so you can see who is approaching.

- Have car keys, house keys, ATM cards, etc. ready so you minimize time you expose your blind side.

- Carry a weapon of some sort—see chapter 4 on weapons—even if it's just a pen. If someone threatens you, go into your "Not me!" mind-set, show the weapon, make eye contact, and get away.

- Stay in Yellow—if someone or someplace doesn't feel right, get away immediately.

- DO NOT GET TRANSPORTED by an attacker.

PREPARATION FOR PARTYING:

- Go with friends you trust and agree on rules before you go:

    - No one leaves with a stranger.

    - No one who has had too much to drink is left alone.

    - Everyone leaves if someone is drugged.

- Do not get separated from the group with a stranger.

- If you didn't see the drink from the bartender's hand to your hand, don't drink it.

- If you think you have been drugged, get with someone you trust immediately or call 911.

- Stay in Yellow. If someone or someplace doesn't feel right, get away immediately.

IF YOU ARE ASSAULTED:

- Report every attack. It's not your fault!

- Call 911 immediately.

- Do not change clothes or clean up—evidence may be affected.

- Do not use the bathroom (if possible)—evidence may be affected.

- Do not eat, smoke, or chew gum—evidence may be affected.

- Write down everything you can remember while it's fresh in your mind:

Car make, model, color, license number.

Race of attacker.

Age, weight, and height

Color of hair

Color of eyes

Clothing

Unusual marks, scars, tattoos, rings, etc.

Facial hair

Odors

- Once the reporting activities are done, get the support and emotional help you need.

THE PERFECT GIFT
for GIRLS *and* WOMEN
YOU CARE ABOUT...

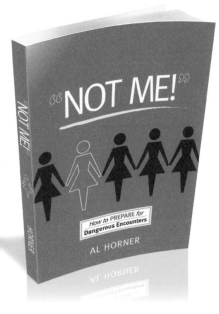

IF YOU ENJOYED THIS BOOK and want to give copies to girls and women you care about, you will find special pricing for multiple book orders at

www.**NOTMEBOOK**.com

If you want to sponsor a gift of Not Me! books to girls in a high school, middle school, athletic teams, churches or any other group you will receive a special sponsor price. It's easy to give this gift of empowering information. Just go to Notmebook.com and click the "Sponsor" tab.

 ## SHARING YOUR VALUABLE KNOWLEDGE...

If you face a dangerous encounter and use the techniques in this book, or other techniques, to win, please consider sharing that valuable experience with other girls and women. Do so using the "I Won" tab at Notmebook.com. See what has worked well for other girls and women on this page.